O9-BTN-474

Entrelac

The Essential Guide to Interlace Knitting

ROSEMARY DRYSDALE

sixth&spring
books

contents

sixth&spring books

161 Avenue of the Americas,
New York, NY 10013

Copyright © 2010
by Rosemary Drysdale

All rights reserved. No part
of this publication may be
reproduced or used in any
form or by any means—
graphic, electronic, or
mechanical, including
photocopying, recording, or
information storage-and-
retrieval systems—without
written permission of the
publisher.

The written instructions,
photographs, designs,
projects and patterns are
intended for the personal,
noncommercial use of the
retail purchaser and are
under federal copyright
laws; they are not to be
reproduced in any form for
commercial use. Permission
is granted to photocopy
patterns for the personal use
of the retail purchaser.

Library of Congress
Control Number:
2010932159

ISBN: 978-1-936096-00-8

Manufactured in China

1 3 5 7 9 10 8 6 4 2

First Edition

notes

■ While all of the yarns used in the
patterns were available at the time of
printing, some of them may have
since been discontinued. To find a
substitute, look at the yarn weight
symbol in the materials list and
choose a yarn that has the same
number. (See page 157 for a table of
standard yarn weights.) Be sure to
knit a gauge swatch and take care
that both the stitch and row gauge
match those listed in the instructions.
Also note that yarn amounts may vary
depending on the weight and yardage
of the substitute yarn.

■ There are many ways to approach
entrelac, and the variety of projects
addresses many different techniques
Follow the patterns carefully.

untangling entrelac

❖The word *entrelac* comes from the French *entrelacer,* which means to interlace. The technique is so named because it resembles a basketweave pattern. The basic pattern is made up of triangles and rectangles that look like slightly elongated diamonds and is usually worked in stockinette stitch. Although entrelac may look tricky, all you need to know for the basic technique is how to cast on, knit, purl, pick up stitches, increase and decrease. However, entrelac can be worked in almost any stitch or color pattern.

I first became interested in entrelac in the 1970s when I was asked by a yarn company to teach an entrelac class. Recently, after a conversation with another designer about entrelac, I began to think about how much potential there is in this technique. I started to explore the possibilities of entrelac and am thrilled to be able to share what I have learned in this book.

To make it as easy as possible, I begin with step-by-step photos and instructions for the basic entrelac technique as well as knitting entrelac in the round and knitting a triangle.

The next section is a stitch dictionary with more than 65 patterns. I've included a little bit of everything, from lace to cables to colorwork designs to beaded and embroidered patterns.

More than 25 complete patterns for sweaters, scarves, wraps, blankets, baby knits and other projects explore the myriad possibilities of incorporating entrelac into design. Finally, for adventurous knitters, I share some tips for designing with entrelac.

I hope you have as much fun discovering this fascinating technique as I have had sharing it with you.❖

entre nous

Throughout this book you will find tip boxes with bits of extra information to make knitting the swatch or garment easier or give you ideas for variations on projects. It's just *entre nous* (between us)!

3

entrelac
step by step

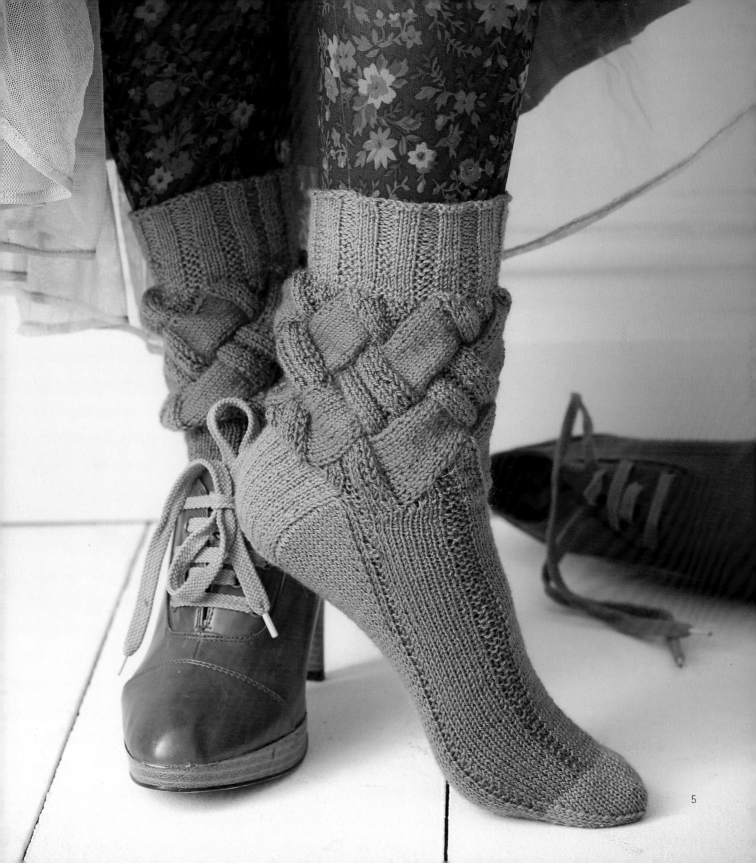

Basics

Picking Up Stitches

Knitting Backward

In the Round

Wrap & Turn

Entrelac Triangle

Basic Entrelac

In this example, you will learn how to create an entrelac swatch that consists of five rows of stockinette-stitch triangles and rectangles. This is the most basic entrelac pattern, and it serves as the starting point for all of the entrelac patterns in this book. (See page 19 for complete written instructions.) Once you get the hang of it, you will be ready to tackle the other patterns and the projects. To make it easier to distinguish between sections, you can use two different colors of yarn as I have done here.

BASE TRIANGLES

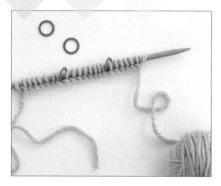

1. Using the method of your choice, cast on 24 stitches. You will be creating 3 Base Triangles, each 8 stitches wide. Place markers at every 8-stitch interval to help distinguish each triangle.

2. To work the first Base Triangle, purl 2 sts on the wrong side of the work. Turn to the right side and k2, turn, p3, turn, k3, turn, p4, turn, k4, turn, p5 (shown here).

3. Turn the work again and k5 on the right side (shown here). Continue in this way, working 1 more stitch every wrong-side row until 8 purl stitches have been worked. Do *not* turn. You are now ready to work a second triangle.

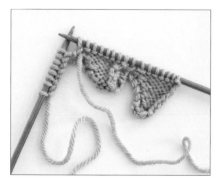

4. Work the second triangle as you did the first. Do *not* turn. You are now ready to start the third base triangle.

5. Work the third triangle as you did the first and second. Turn. You may think you have done something wrong, but this is how it should look—3 triangles that are attached to one another and curl up at the tips. The Base Triangles are now complete. ❖

RIGHT-HAND CORNER TRIANGLE

1. You are now ready to begin the Right-hand (RH) Corner Triangle. (I changed to a darker color yarn for clarity, but you can use the same color.) Knit 2 stitches (shown here) and turn. Purl 2 stitches and turn.

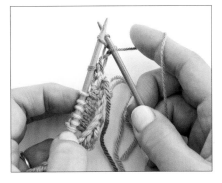

2. On the right side, increase 1 stitch by knitting into the front and then the back (k1fb) of the first stitch.

3. Slip, slip, knit (ssk—see explanation below) with the dark stitch on right-hand needle and the light stitch on left-hand needle of the Base Triangle to decrease 1 stitch (shown here). Turn, p 3 stitches, turn.

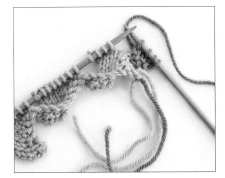

4. K1fb in the first stitch to increase, k1, then work an ssk decrease at the end of the row—there are 4 stitches on the needle, shown here. Turn, p 4 stitches, turn. K1fb, k2, ssk, turn. P5, turn. K1fb, k3, ssk, turn. P6, turn. K1fb, k4, ssk, turn. P7, turn.

5. On the next row, k1fb, k5, ssk in the last stitch of the Base Triangle—8 stitches are on right-hand needle and a Corner Triangle is made. ❖

entre nous

SSK If you are not familiar with this decrease, here's how: Slip 2 sts knitwise, one at a time, to RH needle, insert LH needle into fronts of these 2 sts and knit them together.

RIGHT-SIDE RECTANGLES

1. To begin the first Right-Side (RS) Rectangle, pick up and knit 8 sts down the left side of the first base triangle. (See page 12 for more on picking up stitches.) Turn, purl 8 stitches, turn.

2. To join the first RS Rectangle to the second Base Triangle, knit across the row to the last stitch on the right-hand needle and ssk it with a stitch from the second Base Triangle—a completed ssk shown here. Then turn and purl across the wrong-side row.

3. Repeat until all the stitches from the second Base Triangle are used up.

4. Repeat steps 1 through 3 for the second and third Base Triangles to create two RS Rectangles. You are now ready to begin a Left-Hand (LH) Corner Triangle. ❖

LEFT-HAND CORNER TRIANGLE

1. Pick up and knit 8 stitches along the left-side edge of the last Base Triangle.

2. Decrease stitches on the LH Corner Triangle by working p2tog, then purl across the row. Turn to the right side and knit the remaining stitches. Turn to the wrong side, p2tog, then purl across the row and turn. (Photo shows a p2tog at the beginning of a WS row.)

3. Turn to the right side and knit the remaining stitches.

4. Repeat steps 2 and 3 until two stitches remain on the right side.

5. Turn, purl the last 2 stitches together. If you are using a new color for the next row of rectangles, purl these 2 stitches together with the new color, shown here.

6. Complete the p2tog and one stitch will remain on the needle in the new color. You are now ready to begin the first WS Rectangle. ❖

All you need to know to knit the Silk & Cashmere Cowl on page 84 is the Basic Entrelac technique.

WRONG-SIDE RECTANGLES

1. On the wrong side, pick up and purl 7 stitches down the left-hand side of the LH Corner Triangle.

2. Eight stitches are now on the right-hand needle—7 picked-up stitches plus one stitch that was already on the needle.

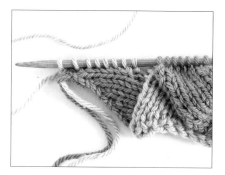

3. Turn and knit 8 stitches.

4. Turn and purl 7 stitches, then p2tog using the last st of the 8 stitches and one from the RS Rectangle.

5. Repeat steps 3 and 4 seven times. Do *not* turn. A Wrong-Side (WS) Rectangle is complete.

6. Rep steps 1 through 5 to create 2 more WS Rectangles. There are no triangles in this row. Work a RH Corner Triangle, a row of RS Rectangles and a LH Corner Triangle. Shown here is step 4 in LH Corner Triangle. Repeat steps 5 and 6. One stitch will remain on the right-hand needle. You can now continue to create as many rows of WS Rectangles and RS Rectangles as you like, always ending with a LH Corner Triangle completed. ❖

END TRIANGLES

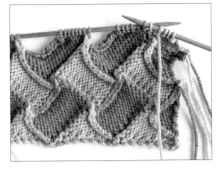

1. Pick up and purl 7 stitches down the side of the LH Corner Triangle, turn. Knit 8 stitches and turn. P2tog at beginning of the WS row, shown here.

2. Purl across the row to the last stitch. Purl together the last stitch of the End Triangle with the first stitch of the RS Rectangle, shown here.

3. After the first End Triangle is complete, pick up and purl 7 stiches down the side of the next rectangle—there are 8 stitches on the right-hand needle, as shown.

4. Repeat steps 1 through 3 to create two more End Triangles. Two stitches remain on the needle.

5. Pass the first stitch over the last stitch to fasten off.

The completed swatch. ❖

Picking Up Stitches

There are several ways to pick up stitches along the side of a triangle or rectangle. Depending on which side of the work is facing, the stitches will either be picked up as knit or purl stitches. Here are a few examples.

1. When working in garter stitch, pick up the stitch in the bump of the stitch and not the space between the bumps.

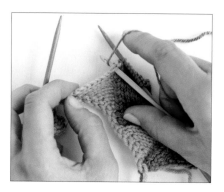

2. A crochet hook may help to make the picking up of the stitches easier. From the knit side, insert hook into the stitch and wrap the yarn around the hook, as shown.

3. Pull a loop through to the front of the work, then slip it on the right-hand needle.

4. From the purl side, insert the hook from back to front into the stitch and wrap the yarn around the hook, as shown.

5. Pull a loop through to the back of the work and slip it on the right-hand needle. ❖

Knitting Backward

Some knitters find the constant turning of the work time-consuming, and sometimes the working yarn starts to curl from all the movement. To avoid the tedium, you can knit back along the right-side row, therefore not doing the purl (wrong-side) row or turning.

1. Work a row of knit in the usual manner from the left-hand needle to the right-hand needle. Do *not* turn the work. With the knit side facing and the yarn in the back, insert the left-hand needle in the back of the next stitch on the right-hand needle, as shown. The right-hand needle will be in front of the stitch.

2. Wrap the yarn around the left-hand needle clockwise. This may seem awkward at first, but as you practice along the row, it will get easier. (**NOTE** You can wrap the yarn counterclockwise, which is a little more difficult, but it will alleviate knitting in the back loop on the following row.)

3. Pull the stitch through the left-hand needle and onto the right-hand needle. Repeat across the row. (**NOTE** If you wrapped the yarn clockwise as shown here, you need to work into the back loop of each stitch to untwist the stitches on the next row.) ❖

entre nous

This sample shows holding the yarn in the right hand, but this technique works just as well for knitters who hold the yarn in their left hand.

Entrelac in the Round

Entrelac can be worked in the round (as in the Fruit and Veggie Caps on page 139). Here are a few tips.

1. After working a row of Base Triangles, cut the yarn and join the round by tying the two ends of the yarn together with the knit side facing out. With a second color, work the first RS Rectangle as you would for the Basic Entrelac, picking up the stitches along the edge of the first triangle.

2. The first RS Rectangle is complete, and you are ready to work the next rectangle. Continue making rectangles between each pair of triangles to complete the round. Turn the work to the wrong side and work the WS Rectangles following the instructions for Basic Entrelac. ❖

Wrap and Turn (w&t)

To avoid holes when working the Base Triangles from an existing piece of knitting, in this case stockinette stitch, you need to use the "wrap and turn" technique. (In the example here, we're knitting in the round.)

1. On the knit side, work to the stitch to be wrapped. With yarn in back, slip the next stitch to the right-hand needle. Move yarn between the needles to the front. Slip the same stitch back to left-hand needle as shown.

2. Bring the yarn to the back again, as shown, and turn to work the next row on the wrong side. One stitch is wrapped.

3. When short rows are done, hide wraps: Work up to wrapped stitch. Insert RH needle under wrap and knitwise into wrapped stitch, as shown. Knit wrap and stitch on needle together.

After wrapping and turning, note the smooth transition between the stockinette-stitch portion and the Base Triangles. ❖

Entrelac Triangle

To knit a triangle-shaped piece in entrelac, you do not create any Base or Corner Triangles. This sample shows two alternating colors to make it easier to see the placement of the rectangles and better demonstrate the technique. For this sample, begin with a single rectangle (labeled #1 in photo) by casting on 8 stitches and working 16 rows in stockinette stitch. Continue to work 10 more rectangles, following the instructions for the Quick-Knit Kerchief (page 113), but working with 8 stitches and 16 rows.

1. Work the next WS Rectangle (#11) by casting on 8 stitches. The sample swatch shows the right side facing for clarity.

2. Continue the WS Rectangle, working p7, p2tog, as shown.

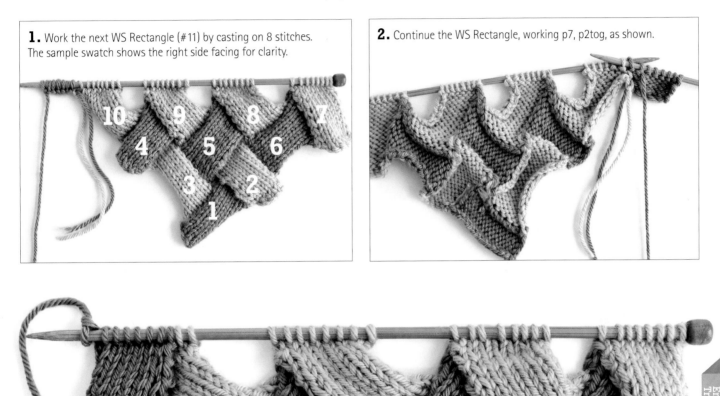

The finished WS Rectangle from the right side. ❖

swatch glossary

Basic

Lace

Cables

Relief

Geometrics

Colorwork

Mélanges

Embroidery

How to Use the Patterns

If you've never worked in entrelac, first practice the basic Stockinette Stitch sample on the opposite page. Once you feel comfortable with the technique, you can try some of the different pattern stitches. When working a cable, lace or other pattern you're not familiar with, first practice just the stitch, then try it in the entrelac pattern. All of the patterns give easy-to-follow directions, so go ahead and knit a few!

Basic Patterns
page 19

This section demonstrates the amazing range of patterns you can create with just knit and purl stitches.

Lace Stitches
page 29

Even the simplest lace patterns add incredible complexity to entrelac. Try them in different yarns for varied effects.

Cable Patterns
page 40

Like lace, cables are an easy way to put entrelac patterns over the top. Any of the ones featured here would make a beautiful design focal point.

Relief Designs
page 44

Bobbles and other textured stitches make these patterns really stand out! Use them as accents in your designs so they don't overpower.

Geometrics
page 50

Entrelac gets graphic when you change the colors of the triangles and rectangles. Use the grid on page 154 to come up with your own designs.

Colorwork
page 56

For even more subtle and complex color effects, you can knit the individual rectangles in stripes or Fair Isle patterns.

Mélanges
page 62

Here we've mixed together a number of techniques and materials—felting, novelty yarns, beads and more.

Embroidery
page 70

Embroidery can add a beautiful touch to entrelac in a number of ways: Use it to outline the rectangles or as accents in centers or at the intersections.

Stockinette Stitch

■ Cast on 24 sts (a multiple of 8).

BASE TRIANGLES
*Row 1 (WS) P2, turn.
Row 2 (RS) K2, turn.
Row 3 P3, turn.
Row 4 K3, turn.
Row 5 P4, turn.
Row 6 K4, turn.
Row 7 P5, turn.
Row 8 K5, turn.
Row 9 P6, turn.
Row 10 K6, turn.
Row 11 P7, turn.
Row 12 K7, turn.
Row 13 P8, do not turn.
Rep from * for two more triangles—3 Base Triangles made. Turn.

RH CORNER TRIANGLE
Row 1 (RS) K2, turn.
Row 2 (WS) P2, turn.
Row 3 Inc in first st by knitting into front and back of st, ssk, turn.
Row 4 P3, turn.
Row 5 Inc in first st, k1, ssk, turn.
Row 6 P4, turn.
Row 7 Inc in first st, k2, ssk, turn.
Row 8 P5, turn.
Row 9 Inc in first st, k3, ssk, turn.
Row 10 P6, turn.
Row 11 Inc in first st, k4, ssk, turn.
Row 12 P7, turn.
Row 13 Inc in first st, k5, ssk, do not turn.
The RH Corner Triangle is complete. Leave 8 sts on RH needle.

RS RECTANGLES
*Pick-up row (RS) Pick up and k 8 sts evenly along edge of next triangle/rectangle, turn.
Row 1 (WS) P8, turn.
Row 2 K7, ssk (with last st of rectangle and first st of next triangle/rectangle), turn.
Rows 3–16 Rep rows 1 and 2 seven times. Do not turn at end of last row.

Rep from * across row—2 RS Rectangles have been worked.

LH CORNER TRIANGLE
Pick-up row (RS) Pick up and k 8 sts along edge of last triangle/rectangle, turn.
Row 1 P2tog, p6, turn.
Row 2 K7, turn.
Row 3 P2tog, p5, turn.
Row 4 K6, turn.
Row 5 P2tog, p4, turn.
Row 6 K5, turn.
Row 7 P2tog, p3, turn.
Row 8 K4, turn.
Row 9 P2tog, p2, turn.
Row 10 K3, turn.
Row 11 P2tog, p1, turn.
Row 12 K2, turn.
Row 13 P2tog, do not turn—1 st remains on RH needle.

**WS RECTANGLES
Pick-up row (WS) Pick up and p 7 sts evenly along edge of triangle just worked—8 sts on RH needle, turn.
*Row 1 K8, turn.
Row 2 P7, p2tog (with last st of rectangle and first st of next triangle/rectangle), turn.
Rows 3–16 Rep rows 1 and 2 seven times. Do not turn.
Next row (WS) Pick up and p 8 sts evenly along edge of next RS rectangle.
Rep from * across row—3 WS Rectangles have been worked. Turn.

Work 1 RH Corner Triangle.
Work 1 row of RS Rectangles.
Do not turn.
Work 1 LH Corner Triangle.
Work a row of WS Rectangles.

NOTE For the sample swatch shown here, this is the last row before the End Triangles. To complete the swatch, work the End Triangles below.
Rep from ** to desired length, ending with a LH Corner Triangle completed—1 st remains on the RH needle. Do not turn.

END TRIANGLES
*Pick-up row (WS) Pick up and p 7 sts evenly along edge of triangle just worked—8 sts on RH needle. Turn.
Row 1 (RS) K8, turn.
Row 2 P2tog, p5, p2tog, turn.
Row 3 K7, turn.
Row 4 P2tog, p4, p2tog, turn.
Row 5 K6, turn.
Row 6 P2tog, p3, p2tog, turn.
Row 7 K5, turn.
Row 8 P2tog, p2, p2tog, turn.
Row 9 K4, turn.
Row 10 P2tog, p1, p2tog, turn.
Row 11 K3, turn.
Row 12 P2tog, p2tog, turn.
Row 13 K2, turn.
Row 14 P2tog, p2tog, pass 1st st over 2nd st—1 st remains on RH needle. Do not turn.
Rep from * across row, picking up sts along edge of rectangle instead of triangle.
Fasten off rem st. ❖

Garter Stitch

- Cast on 24 sts (a multiple of 8).

BASE TRIANGLES
*Row 1 (WS) K2, turn.
Row 2 (RS) K2, turn.
Rows 3 and 4 K3, turn.
Rows 5 and 6 K4, turn.
Rows 7 and 8 K5, turn.
Rows 9 and 10 K6, turn.
Rows 11 and 12 K7, turn.
Row 13 K8, do not turn.
Rep from * for two more triangles
—3 Base Triangles made. Turn.

RH CORNER TRIANGLE
Row 1 (RS) K2, turn.
Row 2 K2, turn.
Row 3 Inc in first st by knitting into front and back of st, ssk, turn.
Row 4 K3, turn.
Row 5 Inc in first st, k1, ssk, turn.
Row 6 K4, turn.
Row 7 Inc in first st, k2, ssk, turn.
Row 8 K5, turn.
Row 9 Inc in first st, k3, ssk, turn.
Row 10 K6, turn.
Row 11 Inc in first st, k4, ssk, turn.
Row 12 K7, turn.
Row 13 Inc in first st, k5, ssk, do not turn.
RH Corner Triangle is complete. Leave 8 sts on RH needle.

RS RECTANGLES
*Pick-up row (RS) Pick up and k 8 sts evenly along edge of next triangle/rectangle, turn.
Row 1 (WS) K8, turn.
Row 2 K7, ssk (with last st of rectangle and first st of next triangle/rectangle), turn.
Rows 3–16 Rep rows 1 and 2 seven times. Do not turn at end of last row.
Rep from * across row—2 RS Rectangles have been worked.

LH CORNER TRIANGLE
Pick-up row (RS) Pick up and k 8 sts along edge of last triangle/rectangle, turn.
Row 1 K2tog, k6, turn.
Row 2 K7, turn.
Row 3 K2tog, k5, turn.
Row 4 K6, turn.
Row 5 K2tog, k4, turn.

Row 6 K5, turn.
Row 7 K2tog, k3, turn.
Row 8 K4, turn.
Row 9 K2tog, k2, turn.
Row 10 K3, turn.
Row 11 K2tog, k1, turn.
Row 12 K2, turn.
Row 13 K2tog, do not turn—1 st remains on needle.

WS RECTANGLES
Pick-up row (WS) Pick up and p 7 sts evenly along edge of triangle just worked, turn.
*Row 1 (RS) P8, turn.
Row 2 P7, p2tog (with last st of rectangle and first st of next triangle/rectangle), turn.
Rows 3–16 Rep rows 1 and 2 seven times. Do not turn.

entre nous

This sample is worked as for the Stockinette Stitch sample (page 19), working in garter stitch for every row. If you pick up and knit, you continue with a knit garter. If you pick up and purl, you continue with a purl garter.

Next row (WS) Pick up and p 8 sts evenly along edge of next RS rectangle. Turn.
Rep from * across row—3 WS Rectangles have been worked. Turn.

**Work 1 RH Corner Triangle. Work 1 row of RS Rectangles. Do not turn.
Work 1 LH Corner Triangle. Work 1 row of WS Rectangles. Rep from ** to desired length, ending with a LH Corner Triangle completed—1 st remains on the needle. Do not turn.

END TRIANGLES
*Pick-up row (WS) Pick up and p 7 sts evenly along edge of triangle just worked. Turn.
Row 1 (RS) P8, turn.
Row 2 P2tog, p5, p2tog, turn.
Row 3 P7, turn.
Row 4 P2tog, p4, p2tog, turn.
Row 5 P6, turn.
Row 6 P2tog, p3, p2tog, turn.
Row 7 P5, turn.
Row 8 P2tog, p2, p2tog, turn.
Row 9 P4, turn.
Row 10 P2tog, p1, p2tog, turn.
Row 11 P3, turn.
Row 12 P2tog, p2tog, turn.
Row 13 P2, turn.
Row 14 P2tog, p2tog, pass 1st st over 2nd st—1 st remains on needle.
Rep from * across row, picking up sts along edge of rectangle instead of triangle.
Fasten off rem st. ❖

Seed Stitch

■ SEED STITCH
Row 1 (RS) *K1, p1; rep from * to end.
Row 2 K the purl sts and p the knit sts.
Rep rows 1 and 2 for seed st.

■ Cast on 21 sts (a multiple of 7).

BASE TRIANGLES
*Row 1 (WS)** P1, k1, turn.
Row 2 (RS) K1, p1, turn.
Rows 3 and 4 P1, k1, p1, turn.
Row 5 [P1, k1] 2 times, turn.
Row 6 [K1, p1] 2 times, turn.
Rows 7 and 8 [P1, k1] 2 times, p1, turn.
Row 9 [P1, k1] 3 times, turn.
Row 10 [K1, p1] 3 times, turn.
Row 11 [P1, k1] 3 times, p1, do *not* turn.
Rep from * for two more triangles —3 Base Triangles made. Turn.

RH CORNER TRIANGLE
Row 1 (RS) P1, k1, turn.
Row 2 K1, p1, turn.
Row 3 Inc in first st by (k1, p1) into st, ssk, turn.

entre nous
When working the "spp" decrease, be sure to pull the next stitch at the beginning of the row tightly.

Row 4 K1, p1, k1, turn.
Row 5 Inc in first st by (p1, k1) into st, p1, ssk, turn.
Row 6 [K1, p1] 2 times, turn.
Row 7 Inc in first st by (k1, p1) into st, k1, p1, ssk, turn.
Row 8 [K1, p1] 2 times, k1, turn.
Row 9 Inc in first st (p1, k1) into st, p1, k1, p1, ssk, turn.
Row 10 [K1, p1] 3 times, turn.
Row 11 Inc in first st by (k1, p1) into st, [k1, p1] 2 times, ssk, do *not* turn.
RH Corner Triangle is complete. Leave 7 sts on RH needle.

RS RECTANGLES
*Pick-up row (RS)** Pick up and k 7 sts evenly along edge of next triangle/rectangle, turn.
Row 1 (WS) [P1, k1] 3 times, p1, turn.
Row 2 [P1, k1] 3 times, spp (with last st of rectangle and first st of next triangle/rectangle), turn.
Rows 3–14 Rep rows 1 and 2 six times. Do *not* turn at end of last row.
Rep from * across row—2 RS Rectangles have been worked.

LH CORNER TRIANGLE
Pick-up row (RS) Pick up and k 7 sts along edge of last triangle/rectangle, turn.
Row 1 (WS) P2tog, [k1, p1] 2 times, k1, turn.
Row 2 [K1, p1] 3 times, turn.
Row 3 K2tog, [p1, k1] 2 times, turn.
Row 4 [K1, p1] 2 times, k1, turn.
Row 5 P2tog, k1, p1, k1, turn.
Row 6 [K1, p1] 2 times, turn.
Row 7 K2tog, p1, k1, turn.
Row 8 K1, p1, k1, turn.
Row 9 P2tog, k1, turn.
Row 10 K1, p1, turn.
Row 11 K2tog, do *not* turn—1 st remains on needle.

WS RECTANGLES
Pick-up row (WS) Pick up and p 6 sts evenly along edge of triangle just worked, turn.
*Row 1 (RS)** [P1, k1] 3 times, p1, turn.
Row 2 [P1, k1] 3 times, spp (with last st of rectangle and first st of next triangle/rectangle), turn.
Rows 3–14 Rep rows 1 and 2 six times. Do *not* turn.
Next row (WS) Pick up and p 7 sts evenly along edge of next RS rectangle.
Rep from * across row—3 WS Rectangles have been worked. Turn.

**Work 1 RH Corner Triangle.
Work 1 row of RS Rectangles.
Do *not* turn.
Work 1 LH Corner Triangle.
Work 1 row of WS Rectangles.
Rep from ** to desired length, ending with a LH Corner Triangle completed—1 st remains on the needle. Do *not* turn.

END TRIANGLES
*Pick-up row (WS)** Pick up and p 6 sts evenly along edge of triangle just worked. Turn.
Row 1 (RS) [P1, k1] 3 times, p1, turn.
Row 2 K2tog, [p1, k1] 2 times, p2tog, turn.
Row 3 [P1, k1] 3 times, turn.
Row 4 P2tog, k1, p1, k1, p2tog, turn.
Row 5 [P1, k1] 2 times, p1, turn.
Row 6 K2tog, p1, k1, p2tog, turn.
Row 7 [P1, k1] 2 times, turn.
Row 8 P2tog, k1, p2tog, turn.
Row 9 P1, k1, p1, turn.
Row 10 K2tog, p2tog, turn.
Row 11 P1, k1, turn.
Row 12 P2tog, k2tog, pass 1st st over 2nd st—1 st remains on needle.
Rep from * across row, picking up sts along edge of rectangle instead of triangle.
Fasten off rem st. ❖

Reverse Stockinette

- Cast on 24 sts (a multiple of 8).

BASE TRIANGLES
*Row 1 (WS) K2, turn.
Row 2 (RS) P2, turn.
Row 3 K3, turn.
Row 4 P3, turn.
Row 5 K4, turn.
Row 6 P4, turn.
Row 7 K5, turn.
Row 8 P5, turn.
Row 9 K6, turn.
Row 10 P6, turn.
Row 11 K7, turn.
Row 12 P7, turn.
Row 13 K8, do *not* turn.
Rep from * for two more triangles —3 Base Triangles made. Turn.

RH CORNER TRIANGLE
Row 1 (RS) P2, turn.
Row 2 K2, turn.
Row 3 Inc in first st by purling into front and back of st, ssp, turn.
Row 4 K3, turn.
Row 5 Inc in first st, p1, ssp, turn.
Row 6 K4, turn.
Row 7 Inc in first st, p2, ssp, turn.
Row 8 K5, turn.
Row 9 Inc in first st, p3, ssp, turn.
Row 10 K6, turn.
Row 11 Inc in first st, p4, ssp, turn.
Row 12 K7, turn.
Row 13 Inc in first st, p5, ssp, do *not* turn.
RH Corner Triangle is complete. Leave 8 sts on RH needle.

RS RECTANGLES
*Pick-up row (RS) Pick up and k 8 sts evenly along edge of next triangle/rectangle, turn.
Row 1 (WS) K8, turn.
Row 2 P7, ssp (with last st of rectangle and first st of next triangle/rectangle), turn.
Rows 3–16 Rep rows 1 and 2 seven times. Do *not* turn at end of last row.
Rep from * across row—2 RS Rectangles have been worked.

LH CORNER TRIANGLE
Pick-up row (RS) Pick up and k 8 sts along edge of last triangle/rectangle, turn.
Row 1 (WS) K2tog, k6, turn.
Row 2 P7, turn.
Row 3 K2tog, k5, turn.
Row 4 P6, turn.
Row 5 K2tog, k4, turn.
Row 6 P5, turn.
Row 7 K2tog, k3, turn.
Row 8 P4, turn.
Row 9 K2tog, k2, turn.
Row 10 P3, turn.
Row 11 K2tog, k1, turn.
Row 12 P2, turn.
Row 13 K2tog, do *not* turn—1 st remains on needle.

WS RECTANGLES
Pick-up row (WS) Pick up and p 7 sts evenly along edge of triangle just worked, turn.
*Row 1 (RS) P8, turn.
Row 2 K7, k2tog (with last st of rectangle and first st of next triangle/rectangle), turn.
Rows 3–16 Rep rows 1 and 2 seven times. Do *not* turn.
Next row (WS) Pick up and p 8 sts evenly along edge of next RS rectangle.
Rep from * across row—3 WS Rectangles have been worked. Turn.

**Work 1 RH Corner Triangle.
Work 1 row of RS Rectangles. Do *not* turn.
Work 1 LH Corner Triangle.
Work 1 row of WS Rectangles.
Rep from ** to desired length, ending with a LH Corner Triangle completed—1 st remains on the needle. Do *not* turn.

END TRIANGLES
*Pick-up row (WS) Pick up and p 7 sts evenly along edge of triangle just worked. Turn.
Row 1 (RS) P8, turn.
Row 2 K2tog, k5, k2tog, turn.
Row 3 P7, turn.
Row 4 K2tog, k4, k2tog, turn.
Row 5 P6, turn.
Row 6 K2tog, k3, k2tog, turn.
Row 7 P5, turn.
Row 8 K2tog, k2, k2tog, turn.
Row 9 P4, turn.
Row 10 K2tog, k1, k2tog, turn.
Row 11 P3, turn.
Row 12 K2tog, k2tog, turn.
Row 13 P2, turn.
Row 14 K2tog, k2tog, pass first st over 2nd st—1 st remains on needle.
Rep from * across row, picking up sts along edge of rectangle instead of triangle.
Fasten off rem st. ❖

entre nous

Even though you might think you should pick up and purl on the RS to correspond to the reverse stockinette stitch pattern, this would make a ridge on the RS. Instead, pick up the stitches as knit sts for a smooth edge, then knit the next WS row to continue the reverse stockinette stitch. The same applies to the picking up of stitches on the WS; that is, pick up and purl the stitches.

Ridge Stitch

■ **RIDGE STITCH ON RS**
Row 1 (RS) Knit.
Row 2 Purl.
Ridge row 3 Purl.
Row 4 Purl.
Rep rows 1–4 for ridge st on RS.

■ **RIDGE STITCH ON WS**
Row 1 (WS) Purl.
Ridge row 2 Purl.
Row 3 Purl.
Row 4 Knit.
Rep rows 1–4 for ridge st on WS.
Cast on 24 sts (a multiple of 8).

BASE TRIANGLES
Work 3 Base Triangles same as for Stockinette Stitch sample (page 19).

RH CORNER TRIANGLE
Work RH Corner Triangle same as for Stockinette Stitch sample.

RS RECTANGLES
*Pick-up row (RS) Pick up and k 8 sts evenly along edge of next triangle/rectangle, turn.
Row 1 (WS) P8 (this is row 2 of ridge pat on the right side), turn.
Row 2 P7, spp (with last st of rectangle and first st of next triangle/rectangle), turn.
Rows 3–16 Rep rows 1 and 2 seven times, keeping in ridge pat (on the right side) as established. Do *not* turn at end of last row.

NOTE On the knit (RS) rows, work skp and on the purl (RS) rows, work spp.
Rep from * across row—2 RS Rectangles have been worked.

LH CORNER TRIANGLE
Work LH Corner Triangle in St st same as for Stockinette Stitch sample.

WS RECTANGLES
Pick-up row (WS) Pick up and p 7 sts evenly along edge of triangle just worked, turn.
*Row 1 (RS) P8 (this is row 2 of ridge pat on the wrong side), turn.
Row 2 P7, p2tog (with last st of rectangle and first st of next triangle/rectangle), turn.
Rows 3–16 Rep rows 1 and 2 seven times, keeping sts in ridge pat (on the wrong side) as established. Do *not* turn.
Next row (WS) Pick up and p 8 sts evenly along edge of next RS Rectangle.
Rep from * across row—3 WS Rectangles have been worked. Turn.

**Work 1 RH Corner Triangle.
Work 1 row of RS Rectangles.
Do *not* turn.
Work 1 LH Corner Triangle.
Work 1 row of WS Rectangles.
Rep from ** to desired length, ending with a LH Corner Triangle completed—1 st remains on the needle. Do *not* turn.

END TRIANGLES
Work 3 End Triangles same as for Stockinette Stitch sample. ❖

23

Stockinette & Seed Stitch

■ SEED STITCH

Row 1 *K1, p1; rep from * to end.
Row 2 K the purl sts and p the knit sts.
Rep row 2 for seed st.

■ Cast on 24 sts (a multiple of 8).

BASE TRIANGLES

Work 3 Base Triangles same as for Stockinette Stitch sample (page 19).

RH CORNER TRIANGLE

Row 1 (RS) K1, p1, turn.
Row 2 P1, k1, turn.
Row 3 Inc in first st by (p1, k1) in next st, p2tog, turn.
Row 4 Work 3 sts in seed st, turn.
Row 5 Inc in first st by (k1, p1) in next st, k1, p2tog, turn.
Row 6 Work 4 sts in seed st, turn.
Row 7 Inc in first st by (p1, k1) in next st, p1, k1, p2tog, turn.
Row 8 Work 5 sts in seed st, turn.
Row 9 Inc in first st by (k1, p1) in next st, k1, p1, k1, p2tog, turn.
Row 10 Work 6 sts in seed st, turn.
Row 11 Inc in first st by (p1, k1) in next st, [p1, k1] twice, p2tog, turn.
Row 12 Work 7 sts in seed st, turn.
Row 13 Inc in first st by (k1, p1) in next st, [k1, p1] twice, k1, p2tog, do *not* turn.
RH Corner Triangle is complete. Leave 8 sts on RH needle.

RS RECTANGLES

***Pick-up row (RS)** Pick up and k 8 sts evenly along edge of next triangle/rectangle, turn.
Row 1 (WS) [P1, k1] 4 times, turn.
Row 2 [K1, p1] 3 times, k1, p2tog (with last st of rectangle and first st of next triangle/rectangle), turn.
Rows 3–16 Rep rows 1 and 2 seven times, keeping sts in seed st as established. Do *not* turn at end of last row.
Rep from * across row–2 RS Rectangles have been worked.

LH CORNER TRIANGLE

Pick-up row (RS) Pick up and k 8 sts along edge of last triangle/rectangle, turn.
Row 1 (WS) P2tog, work 6 sts in seed st, turn.
Row 2 Work 7 sts in seed st, turn.
Row 3 K2tog, work 5 sts in seed st, turn.
Row 4 Work 6 sts in seed st, turn.
Row 5 P2tog, work 4 sts in seed st, turn.
Row 6 Work 5 sts in seed st, turn.
Row 7 K2tog, work 3 sts in seed st, turn.
Row 8 Work 4 sts in seed st, turn.
Row 9 P2tog, work 2 sts in seed st, turn.
Row 10 Work 3 sts in seed st, turn.
Row 11 K2tog, p1, turn.
Row 12 P1, k1, turn.
Row 13 P2tog, do *not* turn–1 st remains on needle.

WS RECTANGLES

Pick-up row (WS) Pick up and p 7 sts evenly along edge of triangle just worked, turn.
***Row 1 (RS)** K8, turn.
Row 2 P7, p2tog (with last st of rectangle and first st of next triangle/rectangle), turn.
Rows 3–16 Rep rows 1 and 2 seven times. Do *not* turn.
Next row (WS) Pick up and p 8 sts evenly along edge of next RS Rectangle.
Rep from * across row–3 WS Rectangles have been worked. Turn.

**Work 1 RH Corner Triangle.
Work 1 row of RS Rectangles. Do *not* turn.
Work 1 LH Corner Triangle.
Work 1 row of WS Rectangles.
Rep from ** to desired length, ending with a LH Corner Triangle completed–1 st remains on the needle. Do *not* turn.

END TRIANGLES

Work 3 End Triangles same as for Stockinette Stitch sample. ❖

Stockinette & Moss Stitch

■ MOSS STITCH
Row 1 *K1, p1; rep from * to end.
Row 2 K the knit sts and p the purl sts.
Row 3 *P1, k1; rep from * to end.
Row 4 K the knit sts and p the purl sts. Rep rows 1–4 for moss st.

■ Cast on 24 sts (a multiple of 8).

BASE TRIANGLES
Work 3 Base Triangles same as for Stockinette Stitch sample (page 19).

RH CORNER TRIANGLE
Work RH Corner Triangle same as for Stockinette Stitch sample.

RS RECTANGLES
*Pick-up row (RS) Pick up and k 8 sts evenly along edge of next triangle/rectangle, turn.
Row 1 (WS) [P1, k1] 4 times, turn.
Row 2 [P1, k1] 3 times, p1, ssk (with last st of rectangle and first st of next triangle/rectangle), turn.
Row 3 [K1, p1] 4 times, turn.
Row 4 [K1, p1] 3 times, k1, p2tog, turn.

Rows 5–16 Rep rows 1 and 2 six times, keeping in moss st as established and working dec as ssk or p2tog to keep to the pattern. Do *not* turn at end of last row.
Rep from * across row—2 RS Rectangles have been worked.

LH CORNER TRIANGLE
Work LH Corner Triangle same as for Stockinette Stitch sample.

WS RECTANGLES
Work WS Rectangles same as for Stockinette Stitch sample.

**Work 1 RH Corner Triangle.
Work 1 row of RS Rectangles.
Do *not* turn.
Work 1 LH Corner Triangle.
Work 1 row of WS Rectangles.
Rep from ** to desired length, ending with a LH Corner Triangle completed—1 st remains on the needle. Do *not* turn.

END TRIANGLES
Work 3 End Triangles same as for Stockinette Stitch sample. ❖

Stockinette & Double Seed Stitch

■ DOUBLE SEED STITCH
Row 1 *K2, p2; rep from * to end.
Row 2 K the knit sts and p the purl sts.
Row 3 *P2, k2; rep from * to end.
Row 4 K the knit sts and p the purl sts. Rep rows 1–4 for double seed st.

■ Cast on 24 sts (a multiple of 8).

BASE TRIANGLES
Work 3 Base Triangles same as for Stockinette Stitch sample (page 19).

RH CORNER TRIANGLE
Work RH Corner Triangle same as for Stockinette Stitch sample.

RS RECTANGLES
*Pick-up row (RS) Pick up and k 8 sts evenly along edge of next triangle/rectangle, turn.
Row 1 (WS) [K2, p2] 2 times, turn.
Row 2 K2, p2, k2, p1, spp (with last st of rectangle and first st of next triangle/rectangle), turn.
Row 3 [P2, k2] 2 times, turn.
Row 4 P2, k2, p2, k1, ssk, turn.

Rows 5–16 Rep rows 1 and 2 six times, keeping in double seed st as established and working dec as ssk or ssp to keep to the pattern. Do *not* turn at end of last row.
Rep from * across row—2 RS Rectangles have been worked.

LH CORNER TRIANGLE
Work LH Corner Triangle same as for Stockinette Stitch sample.

WS RECTANGLES
Work WS Rectangles same as for Stockinette Stitch sample.

**Work 1 RH corner triangle.
Work 1 row of RS Rectangles. Do *not* turn.
Work 1 LH Corner Triangle.
Work 11 row of WS Rectangles.
Rep from ** to desired length, ending with a LH Corner Triangle completed—1 st remains on the needle. Do *not* turn.

END TRIANGLES
Work 3 End Triangles same as for Stockinette Stitch sample. ❖

Stockinette Stitch & K1, P1 Rib

K1, P1 RIB

Row 1 (RS) *K1, p1; rep from * to end.
Row 2 K the knit sts and p the purl sts.
Rep rows 1 and 2 for k1, p1.

Cast on 24 sts (a multiple of 8).

BASE TRIANGLES

Work 3 Base Triangles same as for Stockinette sample (page 19).

RH CORNER TRIANGLE

Work RH Corner Triangle same as for Stockinette Stitch sample.

RS RECTANGLES

*Pick-up row (RS)** Pick up and k 8 sts evenly along edge of next triangle/rectangle, turn.
Row 1 (WS) [P1, k1] 4 times, turn.
Row 2 Rib 7, ssk (with last st of rectangle and first st of next triangle/rectangle), turn.
Rows 3–16 Rep rows 1 and 2 seven times, keeping in k1, p1 rib as established. Do *not* turn at end of last row.
Rep from * across row—2 RS Rectangles have been worked.

LH CORNER TRIANGLE

Work LH Corner Triangle same as for Stockinette Stitch sample.

WS RECTANGLES

Work Rectangles same as for Stockinette Stitch sample.

**Work 1 RH Corner Triangle.
Work 1 row of RS Rectangles. Do *not* turn.
Work 1 LH Corner Triangle.
Work 1 row of WS Rectangles.
Rep from ** to desired length, ending with 1 LH Corner Triangle completed—1 st remains on the needle. Do *not* turn.

End Triangles

Work 3 End Triangles same as for Stockinette Stitch sample. ❖

K2, P2 Rib

Cast on 30 sts (multiple of 10)

BASE TRIANGLES

Work 3 Base Triangles same as for Stockinette Stitch sample (page 19), working 10 sts for each triangle (instead of 8).

RH CORNER TRIANGLE

Work RH Corner Triangle same as for Stockinette Stitch sample, working 10 sts (instead of 8).

RS RECTANGLES

*Pick-up row (RS)** Pick up and k 10 sts evenly along edge of next triangle/rectangle, turn.
Row 1 (WS) [P2, k2] 2 times, p2, turn.
Row 2 [K2, p2] 2 times, k1, ssk (with last st of rectangle and first st of next triangle/rectangle), turn.
Rows 3–20 Rep rows 1 and 2 nine times, keeping in k2, p2 rib. Do *not* turn at end of last row. Rep from * across—2 RS Rectangles worked.

LH CORNER TRIANGLE

Work LH Corner Triangle same as for Stockinette Stitch sample, working 10 sts (instead of 8).

WS RECTANGLES

Pick-up row (WS) Pick up and p 9 sts evenly along edge of triangle just worked, turn.
*Row 1 (RS)** [K2, p2] 2 times, k2, turn.
Row 2 [P2, k2] 2 times, p1, p2tog (with last st of rectangle and first st of next triangle/rectangle), turn.
Rows 3–20 Rep rows 1 and 2 nine times. Do *not* turn.
Next row (WS) Pick up and p 10 sts evenly along edge of next RS rectangle.
Rep from * across row—3 WS Rectangles have been worked. Turn.

**Work a RH Corner Triangle.
Work 1 row of RS Rectangles. Do *not* turn.
Work 1 LH Corner Triangle.
Work 1 row of WS Rectangles.
Rep from ** to desired length, ending with a LH Corner Triangle completed—1 st remains on the needle. Do *not* turn.

END TRIANGLES

Work 3 End Triangles same as for Stockinette Stitch sample, working 10 sts (instead of 8). ❖

Beaded Rib

■ BEADED RIB
Row 1 (RS) *K1, p1; rep from * to end.
Row 2 Purl.
Rep rows 1 and 2 for beaded rib.

■ Cast on 24 sts (a multiple of 8).

BASE TRIANGLES
Work 3 Base Triangles same as for Stockinette Stitch sample (page 19).

RH CORNER TRIANGLE
Work RH Corner Triangle same as for Stockinette Stitch sample.

RS RECTANGLES
*Pick-up row (RS) Pick up and k 8 sts evenly along edge of next triangle/rectangle, turn.
Row 1 (WS) P8, turn.
Row 2 [K1, p1] 3 times, k1, p2tog (with last st of rectangle and first st of next triangle/rectangle), turn.
Rows 3–16 Rep rows 1 and 2 seven times, keeping in beaded rib as established. Do *not* turn at end of last row.
Rep from * across row—2 RS Rectangles have been worked.

LH CORNER TRIANGLE
Work LH Corner Triangle same as for Stockinette Stitch sample.

WS RECTANGLES
Pick-up row (WS) Pick up and p 7 sts evenly along edge of triangle just worked, turn.
*Row 1 (RS) [P1, k1] 4 times.
Row 2 P7, p2tog (with last st of rectangle and first st of next triangle/rectangle), turn.
Rows 3–16 Rep rows 1 and 2 seven times, keeping in beaded rib as established. Do *not* turn.
Next row (WS) Pick up and p 8 sts evenly along edge of next RS rectangle. Turn.
Rep from * across row—3 WS rectangles worked. Turn.

**Work 1 RH Corner Triangle.
Work 1 row of RS Rectangles.
Do *not* turn.
Work 1 LH Corner Triangle.
Work 1 row of WS Rectangles.
Rep from ** to desired length, ending with a LH Corner Triangle completed—1 st remains on the needle. Do *not* turn.

END TRIANGLES
Work 3 End Triangles same as for Stockinette Stitch sample. ❖

Seeded Rib

■ SEEDED RIB
(multiple of 4 sts plus 3)

Row 1 (RS) K1, *p1, k3; rep
from *, end p1, k2.
Row 2 K1, *k3, p1; rep from *,
end k3.
Rep rows 1 and 2 for seeded rib.

Cast on 24 sts (a multiple of 8).

BASE TRIANGLES
Work 3 Base Triangles same as
for Stockinette Stitch sample
(page 19).

RH CORNER TRIANGLE
Work RH Corner Triangle same as
for Stockinette Stitch sample.

RS RECTANGLES
*Pick-up row (RS) Pick up and k
8 sts evenly along edge of next
triangle/rectangle, turn.
Row 1 (WS) K1, p1, k3, p1, k2,
turn.
Row 2 K1, k3, p1, k2, ssk (with
last st of rectangle and first st of
next triangle/rectangle), turn.
Rows 3–16 Rep rows 1 and 2
seven times, keeping in seeded rib
as established. Do *not* turn at end
of last row.
Rep from * across row—2 RS
Rectangles have been worked.

LH CORNER TRIANGLE
Work LH Corner Triangle same as
for Stockinette Stitch sample.

WS RECTANGLES
Pick-up row (WS) Pick up and p
7 sts evenly along edge of
triangle just worked, turn.
*Row 1 (RS) K1, k3, p1, k3.
Row 2 K1, p1, k3, p1, k1, ssk
(with last st of rectangle and first
st of next triangle/rectangle),
turn.
Rows 3–16 Rep rows 1 and 2
seven times, working in seeded
rib. Do *not* turn.
Next row (WS) Pick up and p 8
sts evenly along edge of next RS
Rectangle. Turn.
Rep from * across row—3 WS
Rectangles worked. Turn.

****Work 1 RH Corner Triangle.
Work 1 row of RS Rectangles. Do
not turn.
Work 1 LH Corner Triangle.
Work 1 row of WS Rectangles.
Rep from ** to desired length,
ending with a LH Corner Triangle
completed—1 st remains on the
needle. Do *not* turn.

END TRIANGLES
Work End Triangles same as for
Stockinette Stitch sample. ❖

Basic Faggoting

■ **BASIC FAGGOTING**
(even number of sts)
Row 1 (RS) *K2tog, yo; rep from * to end.
Row 2 Purl.
Rep rows 1 and 2 for basic faggoting.

■ Cast on 24 sts (a multiple of 8).

BASE TRIANGLES
*Row 1 (WS) P2, turn.
Row 2 (RS) K2, turn.
Row 3 P3, turn.
Row 4 K2tog, yo, k1, turn.
Row 5 P4, turn.
Row 6 K2tog, yo, k2, turn.
Row 7 P5, turn.
Row 8 [K2tog, yo] twice, k1, turn.
Row 9 P6, turn.
Row 10 [K2tog, yo] twice, k2, turn.
Row 11 P7, turn.
Row 12 [K2tog, yo] 3 times, k1, turn.
Row 13 P8, do *not* turn.
Rep from * for two more

triangles—3 Base Triangles made. Turn.

RH CORNER TRIANGLE
Row 1 (RS) K2, turn.
Row 2 P2, turn.
Row 3 Inc in first st by knitting into front and back of st, ssk, turn.
Row 4 P3, turn.
Row 5 Inc in first st, k1, ssk, turn.
Row 6 P4, turn.
Row 7 Inc in first st, k2tog, yo, ssk, turn.
Row 8 P5, turn.
Row 9 Inc in first st, k2tog, yo, k1, ssk, turn.
Row 10 P6, turn.
Row 11 Inc in first st, [k2tog, yo] twice, ssk, turn.
Row 12 P7, turn.
Row 13 Inc in first st, [k2tog, yo] twice, k1, ssk, do *not* turn.
RH Corner Triangle is complete. Leave 8 sts on RH needle.

RS RECTANGLES
*Pick-up row (RS) Pick up and k 8 sts evenly along edge of next

triangle/rectangle, turn.
Row 1 (WS) P8.
Row 2 K1, [k2tog, yo] 3 times, ssk (with last st of rectangle and first st of next triangle/rectangle), turn.
Rows 3–16 Rep rows 1 and 2 seven times, working basic faggoting.
Rep from * across row—2 RS Rectangles have been worked.

LH CORNER TRIANGLE
Pick-up row (RS) Pick up and k 8 sts along edge of last triangle/rectangle, turn.
Row 1 (WS) P2tog, p6, turn.
Row 2 [K2tog, yo] 3 times, k1, turn.
Row 3 P2tog, p5, turn.
Row 4 [K2tog, yo] 2 times, k2, turn.
Row 5 P2tog, p4, turn.
Row 6 [K2tog, yo] 2 times, k1, turn.
Row 7 P2tog, p3, turn.
Row 8 K2tog, yo, k2, turn.
Row 9 P2tog, p2, turn.
Row 10 K2tog, yo, k1, turn.
Row 11 P2tog, p1, turn.
Row 12 K2, turn.
Row 13 P2tog, do *not* turn—1 st remains on needle.

WS RECTANGLES
Pick-up row (WS) Pick up and p 7 sts evenly along edge of triangle just worked, turn.
*Row 1 [K2tog, yo] 3 times, k2.
Row 2 P7, p2tog (with last st of rectangle and first st of next triangle/rectangle), turn.
Rows 3–16 Rep rows 1 and 2 seven times, working in basic faggoting. Do *not* turn at end of last row.

Next row (WS) Pick up and p 8 sts evenly along edge of next RS Rectangle.
Rep from * across row—3 WS Rectangles have been worked. Turn.

**Work 1 RH Corner Triangle.
Work 1 row of RS Rectangles. Do not turn.
Work 1 LH Corner Triangle.
Work 1 row of WS Rectangles.
Rep from ** to desired length, ending with a LH Corner Triangle completed—1 st remains on the needle. Do *not* turn.

END TRIANGLES
*Pick-up row (WS) Pick up and p 7 sts evenly along edge of triangle just worked. Turn.
Row 1 (RS) [K2tog, yo] 3 times, k2, turn.
Row 2 P2tog, p5, p2tog, turn.
Row 3 [K2tog, yo] 3 times, k1, turn.
Row 4 P2tog, p4, p2tog, turn.
Row 5 [K2tog, yo] 2 times, k2, turn.
Row 6 P2tog, p3, p2tog, turn.
Row 7 [K2tog, yo] 2 times, k1, turn.
Row 8 P2tog, p2, p2tog, turn.
Row 9 K2tog, yo, k2, turn.
Row 10 P2tog, p1, p2tog, turn.
Row 11 K2tog, yo, k1, turn.
Row 12 P2tog, p2tog, turn.
Row 13 K2, turn.
Row 14 P2tog, p2tog, pass 1st st over 2nd st—1 st remains on needle.
Rep from * across row, picking up sts along edge of rectangle instead of triangle.
Fasten off rem st. ❖

Ridged Eyelet Ribbon with Purl Garter Stitch

■ **RIDGED EYELET RIBBON**
Row 1 (RS) Knit.
Row 2 Purl.
Rows 3 and 4 Knit.
Row 5 *K2tog, yo; rep from *,
end k1.
Row 6 Knit.
Rep rows 1–6 for ridged
eyelet ribbon.

■ Cast on 30 sts (multiple of 10).

BASE TRIANGLES
*Row 1 (WS) P2, turn.
Row 2 (RS) P2, turn.
Rows 3 and 4 P3, turn.
Rows 5 and 6 P4, turn.
Rows 7 and 8 P5, turn.
Rows 9 and 10 P6, turn.
Rows 11 and 12 P7, turn.
Rows 13 and 14 P8, turn.
Rows 15 and 16 P9, turn.
Row 17 P10, do not turn.
Rep from * for two more
triangles—3 Base Triangles made.
Turn.

RH CORNER TRIANGLE
Work RH Corner Triangle same
as for Garter Stitch sample
(page 20), working 10 sts (instead
of 8).

RS Rectangles
*Pick-up row (RS) Pick up and
k 10 sts evenly along edge of
next triangle/rectangle, turn.
**Row 1 (WS) P10, turn.
Row 2 K9, ssk (with last st of
rectangle and first st of next
triangle/rectangle), turn.
Ridge row 3 K10, turn.
Row 4 K2, *k2tog, yo; rep from *
to last 2 sts, k1, ssk, turn.
Ridge row 5 K10, turn.
Row 6 K9, ssk, turn.
Rep from ** 2 times more.
Row 19 P10, turn.
Row 20 K9, ssk. Do not turn.
Rep from * across row—2 RS
Rectangles have been worked.

LH CORNER TRIANGLE
Work LH Corner Triangle same as
for Garter Stitch sample,

working 10 sts (instead of 8).

WS RECTANGLES
Pick-up row (WS) Pick up
and p 9 sts evenly along edge of
triangle just worked, turn.
*Row 1 (RS) K10, turn.
Ridge row 2 K9, ssk (with last
st of rectangle and first st of next
triangle/rectangle), turn.
Row 3 K2, *yo, k2tog; rep from *
to last 2 sts, end k2, turn.
Ridge row 4 K9, ssk, turn.
Row 5 K10.
Row 6 P9, p2tog, turn.
Row 7 K10, turn.
Rep from ** 2 times more.
Row 20 P9, p2tog, do not turn.
Next row (WS) Pick up and
p 10 sts evenly along edge of
next RS Rectangle.
Rep from * across row—3 WS
Rectangles have been worked.
Turn.

**Work 1 RH Corner Triangle.
Work 1 row of RS Rectangles.
Do not turn.

Work 1 LH Corner Triangle.
Work 1 row of WS Rectangles.
Rep from ** to desired length,
ending with a LH Corner Triangle
completed—1 st remains on the
needle. Do not turn.

END TRIANGLES
*Pick-up row (WS) Pick up and
p 9 sts evenly along edge of
triangle just worked. Turn.
Row 1 (RS) P10, turn.
Row 2 P2tog, p7, p2tog, turn.
Row 3 P9, turn.
Row 4 P2tog, p6, p2tog, turn.
Row 5 (RS) P8, turn.
Row 6 P2tog, p5, p2tog, turn.
Row 7 P7, turn.
Row 8 P2tog, p4, p2tog, turn.
Row 9 P6, turn.
Row 10 P2tog, p3, p2tog, turn.
Row 11 P5, turn.
Row 12 P2tog, p2, p2tog, turn.
Row 13 P4, turn.
Row 14 P2tog, p1, p2tog, turn.
Row 15 P3, turn.
Row 16 P2tog, p2tog, turn.
Row 17 P2, turn.
Row 18 P2tog, p2tog,
pass 1st st over 2nd st—1 st
remains on needle.
Rep from * across row, picking
up sts along edge of rectangle
instead of triangle.
Fasten off rem st. ❖

Quadrefoil Eyelet

■ Cast on 30 sts (multiple of 10).

BASE TRIANGLES

Work Base Triangles same as for Stockinette Stitch sample (page 19), working 10 sts for each triangle (instead of 8).

RH CORNER TRIANGLE

Work RH Corner Triangle same as for Stockinette Stitch sample, working 10 sts (instead of 8).

RS RECTANGLES

*Pick-up row (RS) Pick up and k 10 sts evenly along edge of next triangle/rectangle, turn.
Row 1 (WS) P10, turn.
Row 2 K9, ssk, turn.
Row 3 P10, turn.

*Row 4 K5, yo, ssk, k2 ssk (with last st of rectangle and first st of next triangle/rectangle), turn.
Row 5 P10, turn.
Row 6 K3, k2tog, yo, k1, yo, ssk, k1, ssk, turn.
Row 7 P10, turn.
Row 8 K5, yo, ssk, k2, ssk, turn.
Row 9 P10, turn.
Row 10 K9, ssk, turn.
Row 11 P10, turn.*
Rep between *'s once more.
Row 20 K9, ssk, do *not* turn.
Rep from * across row—2 RS Rectangles have been worked.

LH CORNER TRIANGLE

Work LH Corner Triangle same as for Stockinette Stitch sample, working 10 sts (instead of 8).

WS RECTANGLES

Pick-up row (WS) Pick up and p 9 sts evenly along edge of triangle just worked, turn.
Row 1 (RS) K10, turn.
Row 2 P9, p2tog (with last st of rectangle and first st of next triangle/rectangle), turn.
*Row 3 K4, yo, ssk, k4, turn.
Row 4 P9, p2tog, turn.
Row 5 K2, k2tog, yo, k1, yo, ssk, k3, turn.
Row 6 P9, p2tog, turn.
Row 7 K4, yo, ssk, k4, turn.
Row 8 P9, p2tog, turn.
Row 9 K10, turn.
Row 10 P9, p2tog, turn.*
Rep between *'s once more.
Row 19 K10, turn.
Row 20 P9, p2tog, do *not* turn.
Next row (WS) Pick up and p 10

sts evenly along edge of next RS Rectangle.
Rep from * across row—3 WS Rectangles have been worked. Turn.

**Work 1 RH Corner Triangle. Work 1 row of RS Rectangles. Do *not* turn.
Work 1 LH Corner Triangle. Work 1 row of WS Rectangles. Rep from ** to desired length, ending with 1 LH Corner Triangle completed—1 st remains on the needle. Do *not* turn.

END TRIANGLES

Work 3 End Triangles same as for Stockinette Stitch sample, working 10 sts (instead of 8). ❖

Bead Stitch & Garter

■ **BEAD STITCH**
(multiple of 7 sts)

Row 1 (RS) K1, k2tog, yo, k1, yo, ssk, k1.
Row 2 P2tog tbl, yo, p3, yo, p2tog.
Row 3 K1, yo, ssk, k1, k2tog, yo, k1.
Row 4 P2, yo, p3tog, yo, p2.
Rep rows 1–4 for bead st.

■ Cast on 27 sts (multiple of 9).

BASE TRIANGLES
*Row 1 (WS)** P2, turn.
Row 2 (RS) P2, turn.
Rows 3 and 4 P3, turn.
Rows 5 and 6 P4, turn.
Rows 7 and 8 P5, turn.
Rows 9 and 10 P6, turn.
Rows 11 and 12 P7, turn.
Rows 13 and 14 P8, turn.
Row 15 P9, do *not* turn.
Rep from*for two more triangles—3 Base Triangles made. Turn.

RH CORNER TRIANGLE
Work RH Corner Triangle same as for Garter Stitch sample (page 20), working 9 sts (instead of 8).

RS RECTANGLES
*Pick-up row (RS)** Pick up and k 9 sts evenly along edge of next triangle/rectangle, turn.
Row 1 (WS) P9, turn.
Row 2 K1, work row 1 of bead st over 7 sts, ssk (with last st of rectangle and first st of next triangle/rectangle), turn.
Row 3 P1, work row 2 of bead st over 7 sts, p1.
Row 4 K1, work row 3 of bead st over 7 sts, ssk.
Row 5 P1, work row 4 of bead st over 7 sts, p1.
Rows 6–17 Rep rows 2-5 three times.
Row 18 K8, ssk, do *not* turn.
Rep from * across row—2 RS Rectangles have been worked.

LH CORNER TRIANGLE
Work LH Corner Triangle same as for Garter Stitch sample, working 9 sts (instead of 8).

WS RECTANGLES
Pick-up row (WS) Pick up and p 8 sts evenly along edge of triangle just worked, turn.
*Row 1 (RS)** K1, work row 1 of bead st over 7 sts, k1, turn.
Row 2 P1, work row 2 of bead st over 7 sts, p2tog (with last st of rectangle and first st of next triangle/rectangle), turn.
Row 3 K1, work row 3 of bead st over 7 sts, k1, turn.
Row 4 P1, work row 4 of bead st over 7 sts, p2tog, turn.
Rows 5–16 rep rows 1–4 three times.
Row 17 K9, turn.
Row 18 P8, p2tog. Do *not* turn.
Next row (WS) Pick up and p 9 sts evenly along edge of next RS rectangle.

Rep from * across row—3 WS Rectangles have been worked. Turn.

**Work 1 RH Corner Triangle.
Work 1 row of RS Rectangles.
Do *not* turn.
Work 1 LH Corner Tiangle.
Work 1 row of WS Rectangles.
Rep from ** to desired length, ending with a LH Corner Triangle completed—1 st remains on the needle. Do *not* turn.

END TRIANGLES
*Pick-up row (WS)** Pick up and p 8 sts evenly along edge of triangle just worked. Turn.
Row 1 (RS) P9, turn.
Row 2 P2tog, p6, p2tog, turn.
Row 3 P8, turn.
Row 4 P2tog, p5, p2tog, turn.
Row 5 P7, turn.
Row 6 P2tog, p4, p2tog, turn.
Row 7 P6, turn.
Row 8 P2tog, p3, p2tog, turn.
Row 9 P5, turn.
Row 10 P2tog, p2, p2tog, turn.
Row 11 P4, turn.
Row 12 P2tog, p1, p2tog, turn.
Row 13 P3, turn.
Row 14 P2tog, p2tog, turn.
Row 15 P2, turn.
Row 16 P2tog, p2tog, pass 1st st over 2nd st—1 st remains on needle.
Rep from * across row, picking up sts along edge of rectangle instead of triangle.
Fasten off rem st. ❖

Lace Chain

■ **LACE CHAIN STITCH**
Row 1 and all WS rows except row 7 Purl.
Row 2 K2, k2tog, yo, k2tog but do *not* slip from needle, insert RH needle between the sts just worked together and k first st again, then slip both sts from needle tog, yo, ssk, k2.
Row 4 K1, k2tog, yo, k4, yo, ssk, k1.
Row 6 K2tog, yo, k1, k2tog, (yo) twice, ssk, k1, yo, ssk.
Row 7 P4, (k1, p1) into double yo, p to end.
Row 8 K2, yo, ssk, k2, k2tog, yo, k2.
Row 10 K3, yo, ssk, k2tog, yo, k3.
Rep rows 1–10 for lace chain.

■ Cast on 36 sts (multiple of 12).

BASE TRIANGLES
Work 3 Base Triangles same as for Stockinette Stitch sample (page 19), working 12 sts for each triangle (instead of 8).

RH CORNER TRIANGLE
Work RH Corner Triangle same as for Stockinette Stitch sample, working 12 sts (instead of 8).

RS RECTANGLES
*Pick-up row (RS) Pick up and k 12 sts evenly along edge of next triangle/rectangle, turn.
Row 1 (WS) Work row 1 of lace chain over 12 sts, turn.
Row 2 K1, work row 2 of lace chain over 10 sts, ssk (with last st of rectangle and first st of next triangle/rectangle), turn.
Row 3 Work row 3 of lace chain over 12 sts.
Row 4 K1, work row 4 of lace chain over 10 sts, ssk, turn.
Rows 5–24 Rep rows 3 and 4, keeping center 10 sts in lace chain pat as established.

Do *not* turn at end of last row. Rep from * across row—2 RS Rectangles have been worked.

LH CORNER TRIANGLE
Work LH Corner Triangle same as for Stockinette Stitch sample, working 12 sts (instead of 8).

WS RECTANGLES
Pick-up row (WS) Pick up and p 12 sts evenly along edge of triangle just worked, turn.
*Row 1 K1, work row 2 of lace chain over 10 sts, k1, turn.
Row 2 P11, p2tog (with last st of rectangle and first st of next triangle/rectangle), turn.
Rows 3–22 Rep rows 1 and 2, keeping center 10 sts in lace chain pat as established.
Row 23 K12, turn.
Row 24 Rep row 2, do *not* turn.
Next row (WS) Pick up and p 12 sts evenly along edge of next RS Rectangle.
Rep from * across row—3 WS Rectangles have been worked. Turn.

**Work 1 RH Corner Triangle.
Work 1 row of RS Rectangles. Do *not* turn.
Work 1 LH Corner Triangle.
Work 1 row of WS Rectangles.
Rep from ** to desired length, ending with a LH Corner Triangle completed—1 st remains on the needle. Do *not* turn.

END TRIANGLES
Work 3 End Triangles same as for Stockinette Stitch sample, working 12 sts (instead of 8). ❖

Embossed Leaf

■ Cast on 27 sts (multiple of 9).

BASE TRIANGLES
Work 3 Base Triangles same as for Stockinette Stitch sample (page 19), working 9 sts for each triangle (instead of 8).

RH CORNER TRIANGLE
Work RH Corner Triangle same as for Stockinette Stitch sample, working 9 sts (instead of 8).

RS RECTANGLES
*Pick-up row (RS) Pick up and k 9 sts evenly along edge of next triangle/rectangle, turn.
Row 1 (WS) K9, turn.
Row 2 P4, yo, k1, yo, p3, p2tog (with last st of rectangle and first st of next triangle/rectangle), turn.
Row 3 K4, p3, k4, turn.
Row 4 P4, k1, yo, k1, yo, k1, p3, p2tog, turn.
Row 5 K4, p5, k4, turn.

Row 6 P4, k2, yo, k1, yo, k2, p3, p2tog, turn.
Row 7 K4, p7, k4, turn.
Row 8 P4, k3, yo, k1, yo, k3, p3, p2tog, turn.
Row 9 K4, p9, k4, turn.
Row 10 P4, ssk, k5, k2tog, p3, p2tog, turn.
Row 11 K4, p7, k4, turn.
Row 12 P4, ssk, k3, k2tog, p3, p2tog, turn.
Row 13 K4, p5, k4, turn.
Row 14 P4, ssk, k1, k2tog, p3, p2tog, turn.
Row 15 K4, p3, k4, turn.
Row 16 P4, sl 1, k2tog, psso, p3, p2tog, turn.
Row 17 K9, turn.
Row 18 P8, p2tog, do *not* turn.
Rep from * across row—2 RS Rectangles have been worked.

LH CORNER TRIANGLE
Work LH Corner Triangle same as for Stockinette Stitch sample,

working 9 sts (instead of 8).

WS RECTANGLES
Pick-up row (WS) Pick up and p 8 sts evenly along edge of triangle just worked, turn.
*Row 1 (RS) P4, yo, k1, yo, p4, turn.
Row 2 K4, p3, k3, k2tog (with last st of rectangle and first st of next triangle/rectangle), turn.
Row 3 P4, k1, yo, k1, yo, k1, p4.
Row 4 K4, p5, k3, k2tog.
Row 5 P4, k2, yo, k1, yo, k2, p4.
Row 6 K4, p7, k3, k2tog.
Row 7 P4, k3, yo, k1, yo, k3, p4.
Row 8 K4, p9, k3, k2tog.
Row 9 P4, ssk, k5, k2tog, p4.
Row 10 K4, p7, k3, k2tog.
Row 11 P4, ssk, k3, k2tog, p4.
Row 12 K4, p5, k3, k2tog.
Row 13 P4, ssk, k1, k2tog, p4.
Row 14 K4, p3, k3, k2tog.
Row 15 P4, sl 1, k2tog, psso, p4.
Row 16 K8, k2tog.

Row 17 P9.
Row 18 K8, k2tog, do *not* turn.
Next row (WS) Pick up and p 9 sts evenly along edge of next RS Rectangle.
Rep from * across row—3 WS Rectangles have been worked. Turn.

**Work 1 RH Corner Triangle. Work 1 row of RS Rectangles. Do *not* turn.
Work 1 LH Corner Triangle. Work 1 row of WS Rectangles. Rep from ** to desired length, ending with a LH Corner Triangle completed—1 st remains on the needle. Do *not* turn.

END TRIANGLES
Work 3 End Triangles same as for Stockinette Stitch sample, working 9 sts (instead of 8). ❖

Openwork Diamonds

■ Cast on 24 sts (multiple of 8).

BASE TRIANGLES
Work 3 Base Triangles same as for Garter Stitch sample (page 20).

RH CORNER TRIANGLE
Work RH Corner Triangle same as for Garter Stitch sample.

RS RECTANGLES
*Pick-up row (RS) Pick up and k 8 sts evenly along edge of next triangle/rectangle, turn.
Row 1 (WS) K8, turn.
Row 2 K7, ssk (with last st of rectangle and first st of next triangle/rectangle), turn.
Row 3 K8, turn.
Row 4 K2, join 2nd ball of yarn and bind off 4 sts (1 st remains on LH needle), work ssk with this st and next st of next triangle/rectangle, turn.
Row 5 K2, with other ball k2, turn.

Row 6 K2, with other ball k1, ssk, turn.
Row 7 Rep row 5.
Rows 8–11 Rep rows 6 and 7 twice, turn.
Row 12 K2, cast on 4 sts, cut extra ball and using one ball only, k1, ssk, turn.
Row 13 K8, turn.
Row 14 K7, ssk, turn.
Row 15 K8, turn.
Row 16 K7, ssk, do *not* turn.
Rep from * across row—2 RS Rectangles have been worked.

LH CORNER TRIANGLE
Work LH Corner Triangle same as for Garter Stitch sample.

WS RECTANGLES
Pick-up row (WS) Pick up and p 7 sts evenly along edge of triangle just worked—8 sts on needle, turn.

*Row 1 P8, turn.
Row 2 P7, spp (with last st of rectangle and first st of next triangle/rectangle), turn.
Row 3 P8, turn.
Row 4 P2, join 2nd ball of yarn and bind off 4 sts, work spp with last st on needle and next st of next triangle/rectangle, turn.
Row 5 P2, with other ball p2, turn.
Row 6 P2, with other ball p1, spp, turn.
Row 7 Rep row 5.
Rows 8–11 Rep rows 6 and 7 twice—3 sts on LH needle, turn.
Row 12 P2, cast on 4 sts, p1, spp, turn.
Row 13 P8, turn.
Row 14 P7, spp, turn.
Row 15 P8, turn.
Row 16 P7, spp, do *not* turn.
Next row (WS) Pick up and p 8 sts evenly along edge of next RS Rectangle.
Rep from * across row—3 WS

Rectangles have been worked. Turn.

**Work 1 RH Corner Triangle.
Work 1 row of RS Rectangles. Do *not* turn.
Work 1 LH Corner Triangle.
Work 1 row of WS Rectangles.
Rep from ** to desired length, ending with a LH Corner Triangle completed—1 st remains on the needle. Do *not* turn.

End Triangles
Work 3 End Triangles same as for Garter Stitch sample. ❖

entre nous
Although this is not a lace pattern per se, it is a great way to incorporate openwork into an entrelac pattern.

Little Arrowhead Lace

■ **LITTLE ARROWHEAD LACE**
(Panel of 7 sts)

Rows 1 and 3 (WS) Purl.
Row 2 K1, yo, ssk, k1, k2tog, yo, k1.
Row 4 K2, yo, sl 2 knitwise, k1, p2sso, yo, k2.
Rep rows 1–4 for little arrowhead lace.

■ Cast on 30 sts (multiple of 10).

BASE TRIANGLES
Work Base Triangles same as for Stockinette Stitch sample (page 19), working 10 sts for each triangle (instead of 8).

RH CORNER TRIANGLE
Work RH Corner Triangle same as for Stockinette Stitch sample, working 10 sts (instead of 8).

RS RECTANGLES
*Pick-up row (RS) Pick up and k 10 sts evenly along edge of next triangle/rectangle, turn.
Row 1 (WS) P10, turn.
Row 2 K3, yo, ssk, k1, k2tog, yo, k1, ssk (with last st of rectangle and first st of next triangle/rectangle), turn.
Row 3 P10.
Row 4 K4, yo, sl 2 knitwise, k1, p2sso, yo, k2, ssk.
Rows 5–20 Rep rows 1-4 four

times. Do *not* turn at end of last row.
Rep from * across row—2 RS Rectangles have been worked.

LH CORNER TRIANGLE
Work LH Corner Triangle same as for Stockinette Stitch sample, working 10 sts (instead of 8).

WS RECTANGLES
Pick-up row (WS) Pick up and p 9 sts evenly along edge of triangle just worked, turn.
*Row 1 (RS) K2, yo, ssk, k1, k2tog, yo, k3, turn.
Row 2 P9, p2tog (with last st of rectangle and first st of next triangle/rectangle), turn.
Row 3 K3, yo, sl 2 knitwise, k1, p2sso, yo, k4, turn.
Row 4 P9, p2tog, turn.
Rows 5–20 Rep rows 1-4 four

times. Do *not* turn at end of last row.
Next row (WS) Pick up and p 10 sts evenly along edge of next RS Rectangle.
Rep from * across row—3 WS Rectangles have been worked. Turn.

**Work 1 RH Corner Triangle.
Work 1 row of RS Rectangles. Do *not* turn.
Work 1 LH Corner Triangle.
Work 1 row of WS Rectangles.
Rep from ** to desired length, ending with a LH Corner Triangle completed—1 st remains on the needle. Do *not* turn.

End Triangles
Work 3 End Triangles same as for Stockinette Stitch sample, picking up 9 sts (instead of 7). ❖

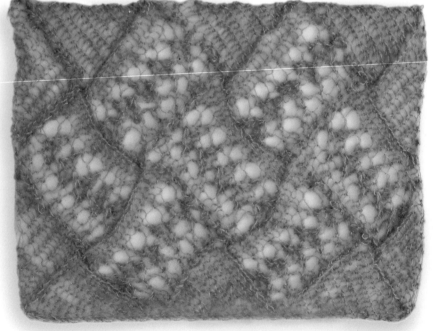

■ One pattern two ways: DK weight wool/polyester (top) and laceweight mohair (bottom).

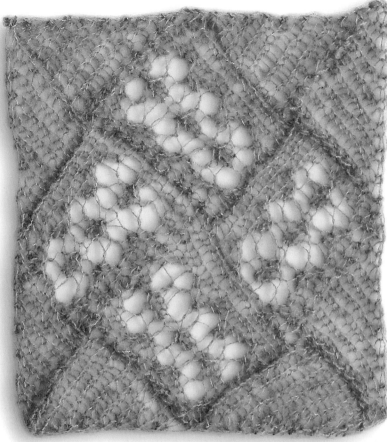

Cat's Paw

triangle just worked, turn—10 sts on needle.
*Row 1 (RS) K1, work row 2 of cat's paw over the next 7 sts, k2, turn.
Row 2 P9, p2tog (with last st of rectangle and first st of next triangle/rectangle), turn.
Row 3 K1, work row 4 of cat's paw over the next 7 sts, k2, turn.
Row 4 P9, p2tog, turn.
Row 5 K1, work row 6 of cat's paw over the next 7 sts, k2.
Row 6 P9, p2tog, turn.
Rows 7–18 Rep rows 1–6 two times
Row 19 K10, turn.
Row 20 P9, p2tog. Do *not* turn.
Next row (WS) Pick up and p 10 sts evenly along edge of next RS Rectangle.
Rep from * across row—2 WS Rectangles have been worked. Turn.

****Work 1 RH Corner Triangle.
Work 1 row of RS Rectangles. Do *not* turn.
Work 1 LH Corner Triangle.
Work 1 row of WS Rectangles.
Rep from ** to desired length, ending with a LH Corner Triangle completed—1 st remains on the needle. Do *not* turn.

END TRIANGLES

Work 2 End Triangles same as for Stockinette Stitch sample, picking up 9 sts (instead of 7)—10 sts on needle. ❖

■ CAT'S PAW
(Panel of 7 sts)

Rows 1, 3 and 5 (WS) Purl.
Row 2 K1, k2tog, yo, k1, yo, ssk, k1.
Row 4 K2tog, yo, k3, yo, ssk.
Row 6 K2, yo, SK2P, yo, k2.
Rep rows 1–6 for cat's paw.

■ Cast on 20 sts (multiple of 10)

BASE TRIANGLES

Work two Base Triangles same as for Stockinette Stitch sample (page 19), working 10 sts for each triangle (instead of 8).

RH CORNER TRIANGLE

Work RH Corner Triangle same as for Stockinette Stitch sample, working 10 sts (instead of 8).

RS RECTANGLES

Pick up row (RS) Pick up and k 10 sts evenly along edge of next triangle/rectangle, turn.
Row 1 (WS) P10, turn.
Row 2 K2, work row 2 of cat's paw over next 7 sts, ssk (with last st of rectangle and first st of next triangle/rectangle), turn.
Row 3 P10, turn.
Row 4 K2, work row 4 of cat's paw over the next 7 sts, ssk, turn.
Row 5 P10, turn.
Row 6 K2, work row 6 of cat's paw over the next 7 sts, ssk, turn.
Rows 7–18 Rep rows 1–6 three times.
Row 19 P10, turn.
Row 20 K9, ssk—1 RS rectangle has been worked.

LH CORNER TRIANGLE

Work LH Corner Triangle same as for Stockinette Stitch sample, working 10 sts (instead of 8).

WS RECTANGLES

Pick-up row (WS) Pick up and p 9 sts evenly along edge of

Gull Wings

■ GULL WINGS
(Panel of 7 sts)

Rows 1 and 3 (WS) Purl.
Row 2 K1, k2tog, yo, k1, yo, ssk, k1.
Row 4 K2tog, yo, k3, yo, ssk.
Rep rows 1–4 for gull wings pat.

■ Cast on 18 sts (multiple of 9).

BASE TRIANGLES
Work 2 Base Triangles same as for Stockinette Stitch sample (page 19), working 9 sts for each triangle (instead of 8).

RH CORNER TRIANGLE
Work RH Corner Triangle same as for Stockinette Stitch sample, working 9 sts (instead of 8).

RS RECTANGLES
*Pick-up row (RS) Pick up and k 9 sts evenly along edge of next triangle/rectangle, turn.
Row 1 (WS) P9, turn.
Row 2 K1, work row 2 of gull wings pat over next 7 sts, ssk (with last st of rectangle and first st of next triangle/rectangle), turn.
Row 3 P9, turn.
Row 4 K1, work row 4 of gull wings pat over next 7 sts, ssk, turn.
Rows 5–16 Rep rows 1–4 three times.
Row 17 P9, turn.
Row 18 K8, ssk, do *not* turn. Rep from * across row—1 RS Rectangle has been worked.

LH CORNER TRIANGLE
Work LH Corner Triangle same as for Stockinette Stitch sample, working 9 sts (instead of 8).

WS RECTANGLES
Pick-up row (WS) Pick up and p 8 sts evenly along edge of triangle just worked, turn—9 sts on needle.
*Row 1 (RS) K1, work row 2 of gull wings pat over next 7 sts, k1, turn.
Row 2 P8, p2tog (with last st of rectangle and first st of next triangle/rectangle), turn.
Row 3 K1, work row 4 of gull wings pat over next 7 sts, k1, turn.
Row 4 P8, p2tog (with last st of rectangle and first st of next triangle/rectangle), turn.
Rows 5–16 Rep rows 1–4 three times.
Row 17 K9, turn.
Row 18 P8, p2tog. Do *not* turn.
Next row (WS) Pick up and p 9 sts evenly along edge of next RS rectangle.
Rep from * across row—2 WS Rectangles have been worked. Turn.

****Work 1 RH Corner Triangle. Work 1 row of RS Rectangles. Do *not* turn.
Work 1 LH Corner Triangle. Work 1 row of WS Rectangle. Rep from ** to desired length, ending with a LH Corner Triangle completed—1 st remains on the needle. Do *not* turn.

END TRIANGLES
Work 2 End Triangles same as for Stockinette Stitch sample, picking up 8 sts (instead of 7)—9 sts on needle. ❖

Bat Wing Lace

■ BAT WING LACE
(Panel of 12 sts)

Row 1 (RS) K3, [k2tog, yo] twice, ssk, k3.
Row 2 P2, p2tog tbl, yo, p1, p in front and back of next st, p1, yo, p2tog, p2.
Row 3 K1, k2tog, yo, k6, yo, ssk, k1.
Row 4 P2tog tbl, yo, p8, yo, p2tog.
Row 5 K1, yo, k3, k2tog, ssk, k3, yo, k1.
Row 6 P2, yo, p2, p2tog tbl, p2tog, p2, yo, p2.
Row 7 K3, yo, k1, k2tog, ssk, k1, yo, k3.
Row 8 P4, yo, p2tog tbl, p2tog, yo, p4.
Rep rows 1–8 for bat wing lace pat.

■ Cast on 28 sts (multiple of 14).

BASE TRIANGLES
Work 2 Base Triangles same as for Stockinette Stitch sample (page 19), working 14 sts for each triangle (instead of 8).

RH CORNER TRIANGLE
Work RH Corner Triangle same as for Stockinette Stitch sample, working 14 sts (instead of 8).

RS RECTANGLES
*Pick-up row (RS) Pick up and k 14 sts evenly along edge of next triangle/rectangle, turn.
Row 1 (WS) P14, turn.
Row 2 K1, work row 1 of lace pat over next 12 sts, ssk (with last st of rectangle and first st of next

st of rectangle and first st of next triangle/rectangle), turn.

Row 3 K1, work row 3 of lace pat over next 12 sts, k1, turn.

Row 4 P1, work row 4 of lace pat over next 12 sts, p2tog, turn.

Row 5 K1, work row 5 of lace pat over next 12 sts, k1, turn.

Row 6 P1, work row 6 of lace pat over next 12 sts, p2tog, turn.

Row 7 K1, work row 7 of lace pat over next 12 sts, k1, turn.

Row 8 P1, work row 8 of lace pat over next 12 sts, p2tog, turn.

Rows 9–24 Rep rows 1–8 two times.

Row 25 K14, turn.

Row 26 P13, p2tog, turn.

Row 27 K14, turn.

Row 28 P13,. P2tog, do *not* turn.

Next row (WS) Pick up and p 14 sts evenly along edge of next RS Rectangle.

Rep from * across row—2 WS Rectangles have been worked. Turn.

**Work 1 RH Corner Triangle.
Work 1 row of RS Rectangles. Do *not* turn.
Work 1 LH Corner Triangle.
Work 1 row of WS Rectangles.
Rep from ** to desired length, ending with a LH Corner Triangle completed—1 st remains on the needle. Do *not* turn.

END TRIANGLES

Work 2 End Triangles same as for Stockinette Stitch sample, picking up 13 sts (instead of 7)—14 sts on needle.❖

■ Both Gull Wings and Bat Wing Lace were made using a lace-weight mohair yarn.

triangle/rectangle), turn.

Row 3 P1, work row 2 of lace pat over next 12 sts, p1, turn.

Row 4 K1, work row 3 of lace pat over next 12 sts, ssk, turn.

Row 5 P1, work row 4 of lace pat over next 12 sts, p1, turn.

Row 6 K1, work row 5 of lace pat over next 12 sts, ssk, turn.

Row 7 P1, work row 6 of lace pat over next 12 sts, p1, turn.

Row 8 K1, work row 7 of lace pat over next 12 sts, ssk, turn.

Row 9 P1, work row 8 of lace pat over next 12 sts, p1, turn.

Rows 10–25 Rep rows 2–9 two times.

Row 26 K13, ssk, turn.

Row 27 P14, turn.

Row 28 K13, ssk, do *not* turn—1 RS Rectangle has been worked.

LH CORNER TRIANGLE

Work LH Corner Triangle same as for Stockinette Stitch sample, picking up 13 sts (instead of 7)— 14 sts on needle.

WS RECTANGLES

Pick-up row (WS) Pick up and p 14 sts evenly along edge of triangle just worked, turn.

*Row 1 (RS) K1, work row 1 of lace pat over next 12 sts, k1, turn.

Row 2 P1, work row 2 of lace pat over next 12 sts, p2tog (with last

Scotch Faggoting Cable

■ **SCOTCH FAGGOTING CABLE**
(Panel of 8 sts)

Row 1 (RS) P2, k2, yo, k2tog, p2.
Row 2 K2, p2, yo, p2tog, k2.
Rows 3, 5 and 7 Rep row 1.
Rows 4 and 6 Rep row 2.
Row 9 P2, sl 2 to cn and hold to *front*, k2, k2 from cn, p2.
Row 8 Rep row 2.
Rows 11, 13 and 15 Rep row 1.
Rows 10, 12, 14 and 16
Rep row 2.
Rep rows 1–16 for scotch faggoting cable.

Cast on 24 sts (a multiple of 8).

BASE TRIANGLES

Work 3 Base Triangles same as for Stockinette Stitch sample (page 19).

RH CORNER TRIANGLE

Work RH Corner Triangle same as for Stockinette Stitch sample.

RS RECTANGLES

***Pick-up row (RS)** Pick up and k 8 sts evenly along edge of next triangle/rectangle, turn.
Row 1 Work row 2 of cable pat.
Row 2 Work row 3 of cable pat over 7 sts, spp (with last st of rectangle and first st of next triangle/rectangle), turn.
Rows 3–17 Rep rows 1 and 2 seven times, then rep row 1 once more, keeping in cable pat as established. Do *not* turn at end of last row.
Rep from * across row—2 RS Rectangles have been worked.

LH CORNER TRIANGLE

Work LH Corner Triangle same as for Stockinette Stitch sample.

WS RECTANGLES

Pick-up row (WS) Pick up and p 7 sts evenly along edge of triangle just worked, turn.
***Row 1 (RS)** Work row 15 of cable pat.

Row 2 Work row 2 of cable pat over 7 sts, ssk (with last st of rectangle and first st of next triangle/rectangle), turn.
Rows 3–16 Rep rows 1 and 2 seven times, keeping in cable pat as established. Do *not* turn at end of last row.
Next row (WS) Pick up and p 8 sts evenly along edge of next RS Rectangle.
Rep from * across row—3 WS Rectangles have been worked. Turn.

**Work 1 RH Corner Triangle.
Work 1 row of RS Rectangles.
Do *not* turn.
Work 1 LH Corner Triangle.
Work 1 row of WS Rectangles.
Rep from ** to desired length, ending with a LH Corner Triangle completed—1 st remains on the needle. Do *not* turn.

END TRIANGLES

Work 3 End Triangles same as for Stockinette Stitch sample. ❖

Horseshoe Cable

■ **HORSESHOE CABLE PANEL**
(Over 8 sts)

Row 1 (RS) K8.
Rows 2 and 4 P8.
Row 3 Sl 2 sts to cn and hold to *front*, k2, k2 from cn, sl 2 sts to cn and hold to back, k2, k2 from cn.
Rep rows 1–4 for horseshoe cable panel.

■ Cast on 42 sts (multiple of 14).

BASE TRIANGLES

Work 3 Base Triangles same as for Stockinette Stitch sample (page 19), working 14 sts for each triangle (instead of 8).

RH CORNER TRIANGLE

Work RH Corner Triangle same as for Stockinette Stitch sample, working 14 sts (instead of 8).

RS RECTANGLES

***Pick-up row (RS)** Pick up and k 14 sts evenly along edge of next triangle/rectangle, turn.
Row 1 (WS) K3, p8, k3, turn.
Row 2 P3, work row 1 of horseshoe cable panel over 8 sts, p2, spp (with last st of rectangle and first st of next triangle/rectangle), turn.
Row 3 K3, work row 2 of horseshoe cable over 8 sts, k3.
Row 4 P3, work row 3 of horseshoe cable over 8 sts, p2, spp.
Row 5 K3, work row 4 of horseshoe cable over 8 sts, k3.

Rows 6–28 Rep rows 2–5, keeping center 8 sts in horseshoe cable as established. Do *not* turn at end of last row.
Rep from * across row—2 RS Rectangles have been worked.

LH CORNER TRIANGLE
Work LH Corner Triangle same as for Stockinette Stitch sample, working 14 sts (instead of 8).

WS RECTANGLES
Pick-up row (WS) Pick up and p 13 sts evenly along edge of triangle just worked—14 sts on RH needle. Turn.
***Row 1 (RS)** P3, work row 1 of horseshoe cable over 8 sts, p3, turn.
Row 2 K3, work row 2 of horseshoe cable over 8 sts, k2, ssk (with last st of rectangle and first st of next triangle/rectangle), turn.
Rows 3–28 Rep rows 1 and 2, keeping center 8 sts in horseshoe cable as established.

Do *not* turn at end of last row.

Next row (WS) Pick up and p 14 sts evenly along edge of next RS Rectangle.
Rep from * across row—3 WS Rectangles have been worked. Turn.

**Work 1 RH Corner Triangle. Work 1 row of RS Rectangles. Do *not* turn. Work 1 LH Corner Triangle. Work 1 row of WS Rectangles.

Rep from ** to desired length, ending with a LH Corner Triangle completed—1 st remains on the needle. Do *not* turn.

END TRIANGLES
Work 3 End Triangles same as for Stockinette Stitch sample, working 14 sts (instead of 8). ❖

4-Stitch Cable Panel

■ LEFT CABLE PANEL
(Over 8 sts)
Rows 1, 3 and 5 (WS) K2, p4, k2.
Cable row 2 P2, sl 2 sts to cn and hold to *front*, k2, k2 from cn, p2.
Row 4 P2, k4, p2.
Rep rows 1–4 for left cable panel.

■ RIGHT CABLE PANEL
(Over 8 sts)
Rows 1 and 3 (WS) K2, p4, k2.
Cable row 2 P2, sl 2 sts to cn and hold to *back*, k2, k2 from cn, p2.
Row 4 P2, k4, p2.
Rep rows 1–4 for left cable panel.

■ Cast on 42 sts (multiple of 14)

BASE TRIANGLES
Work 3 Base Triangles same as for Stockinette Stitch sample (page 19), working 14 sts for each triangle (instead of 8).

RH CORNER TRIANGLE
Work RH Corner Triangle same as for Stockinette Stitch sample, working 14 sts (instead of 8).

RS RECTANGLES
*Pick-up row (RS) Pick up and k 14 sts evenly along edge of next triangle/rectangle, turn.
Row 1 (WS) P3, work row 1 of left cable panel over 8 sts, p3, turn.
Row 2 K3, work row 2 of left cable panel over 8 sts, k2, ssk (with last st of rectangle and first st of next triangle/rectangle), turn.
Row 3 P3, work row 3 of left cable panel over 8 sts, p3.
Row 4 K3, work row 4 of left cable panel over 8 sts, k2, ssk.
Rows 5–28 Rep rows 1–4, keeping center 8 sts in left cable panel as established.
Do *not* turn at end of last row.
Rep from * across row—2 RS Rectangles have been worked.

LH CORNER TRIANGLE
Work LH Corner Triangle same as for Stockinette Stitch sample, working 14 sts (instead of 8).

WS RECTANGLES
Pick-up row (WS) Pick up and p 13 sts evenly along edge of triangle just worked, turn.
*Row 1 (RS) K3, work row 2 of right cable panel over 8 sts, k3, turn.
Row 2 P3, work row 3 of right cable panel over 8 sts, p2, p2tog (with last st of rectangle and first st of next triangle/rectangle), turn.
Rows 3–28 Rep rows 1 and 2, keeping center 8 sts in right cable panel as established. Do *not* turn at end of last row.
Next row (WS) Pick up and p 14 sts evenly along edge of next RS Rectangle.
Rep from * across row—3 WS Rectangles have been worked.
Turn.

****Work 1 RH Corner Triangle.
Work 1 row of RS Rectangles. Do *not* turn.
Work 1 LH Corner Triangle.
Work 1 row of WS Rectangles.
Rep from ** to desired length, ending with a LH Corner Triangle completed—1 st remains on the needle. Do *not* turn.

END TRIANGLES
Work 3 End Triangles same as for Stockinette Stitch sample, working 14 sts (instead of 8). ❖

Aran Diamond

stitches

3-st BC Slip 1 st to cn and hold to *back*, k2, k1 from cn.
3-st FC Slip 2 sts to cn and hold to *front*, k1, k2 from cn.
3-st BPC Slip 1 st to cn and hold to *back*, k2, p1 from cn.
3-st FPC Slip 2 sts to cn and hold to *front*, p1, k2 from cn.
4-st BC Slip 2 sts to cn and hold to *back*, k2, k2 from cn.
4-st FC Slip 2 sts to cn and hold to *front*, k2, k2 from cn.

NOTE Be sure to pull the sts of the decrease as tightly as possible for a neat edge.

■ Cast on 28 sts (multiple of 14).

Work same as Garter Stitch sample (page 20).

BASE TRIANGLES
Work 2 Base Triangles in knit garter same as Garter Stitch sample, working 14 sts (instead of 8).

RH CORNER TRIANGLE
Work RH Corner Triangle in knit garter same as Garter Stitch sample, working 14 sts (instead of 8).

RS RECTANGLES
*Pick-up row (RS) Pick up and k 14 sts evenly along edge of next triangle/rectangle, turn.
Row 1 (WS) K14, turn.

Cables

LH CORNER TRIANGLE

Work LH Corner Triangle in knit garter same as Garter Stitch sample, working 14 sts (instead of 8).

WS RECTANGLES

*Pick-up row (WS) Pick up and p 13 sts evenly along edge of triangle just worked—14 sts on needle, turn.

Row 1 (RS) P14, turn.

Row 2 K13, ssk (with last st of rectangle and first st of next triangle/rectangle), turn.

Row 3 P5, k4, p5, turn.

Row 4 K5, p4, k4, ssk, turn.

Row 5 P5, 4-st BC, p5, turn.

Row 6 K5, p4, k4, ssk, turn.

Row 7 P4, 3-st BC, 3-st FC, p4, turn.

Row 8 K4, p2, k2, p2, k3, ssk, turn.

Row 9 P3, 3-st BC, k2, 3-st FC, p3, turn.

Row 10 K3, p2, k4, p2, k2, ssk, turn.

Row 11 P2, 3-st BC, k4, 3-st FC, p2, turn.

Row 12 K2, p2, k6, p2, k1, ssk, turn.

Row 13 P1, 3-st BC, k6, 3-st FC, p1, turn.

Row 14 K1, p2, k8, p2, ssk, turn.

Row 15 P1, k12, p1, turn.

Row 16 Rep row 14, turn.

Row 17 P1, 3-st FPC, k6, 3-st BPC, p1, turn.

Row 18 Rep row 12, turn.

Row 19 P2, 3-st FPC, k4, 3-st BPC, p2, turn.

Row 20 Rep row 10, turn.

Row 21 P3, 3-st FPC, k2, 3-st BPC, p3, turn.

Row 22 Rep row 8, turn.

Row 23 P4, 3-st FPC, 3-st BPC, p4, turn.

Row 24 Rep row 6, turn.

Row 25 P5, 4-st BC, p5, turn.

Row 26 K13, ssk, turn.

Row 27 P14, turn.

Row 28 K13, ssk. Do *not* turn.

Rep from * once more. 2 WS Rectangles have been worked. Turn.

**Work 1 RH Corner Triangle. Work 1 row of RS Rectangles. Do *not* turn. Work 1 LH Corner Triangle. Work 1 row of WS Rectangles. Rep from ** to desired length, ending with a LH Corner Triangle completed—1 st remains on the needle. Do *not* turn.

END TRIANGLES

Work 2 End Triangles in knit garter same as Garter Stitch sample, picking up 13 sts (instead of 7). ❖

entre nous

This design makes a great allover pattern that creates a counterpane effect—cast on more stitches for an heirloom blanket for the new baby.

Row 2 P13, spp (with last st of rectangle and first st of next triangle/rectangle), turn.

Row 3 K14, turn.

Begin Aran Diamond

Row 4 P5, k4, p4, spp, turn.

Row 5 K5, p4, k5, turn.

Row 6 P5, 4-st BC, p4, spp, turn.

Row 7 Rep row 5, turn.

Row 8 P4, 3-st BC, 3-st FC, p3, spp, turn.

Row 9 K4, p2, k2, p2, k4, turn.

Row 10 P3, 3-st BC, k2, 3-st FC, p2, spp.

Row 11 K3, p2, k4, p2, k3, turn.

Row 12 P2, 3-st BC, k4, 3-st FC, p1, spp, turn.

Row 13 K2, p2, k6, p2, k2, turn.

Row 14 P1, 3-st BC, k6, 3-st FC, spp, turn

Row 15 K1, p2, k8, p2, k1, turn.

Row 16 P1, k12, spp, turn.

Row 17 Rep row 15, turn.

Row 18 P1, 3-st FPC, k6, 3-st BPC, spp, turn.

Row 19 Rep row 13, turn.

Row 20 P2, 3-st FPC, k4, 3-st BPC, p1, spp.

Row 21 Rep row 11, turn.

Row 22 P3, 3-st FPC, k2, 3-st BPC, p2, spp, turn.

Row 23 Rep row 9, turn.

Row 24 P4, 3-st FPC, 3-st BPC, p3, spp, turn.

Row 25 Rep row 5, turn.

Row 26 Rep row 6, turn.

Row 27 K14, turn.

Row 28 P13, spp, turn. Do *not* turn.

Rep from * across row—1 RS Rectangle has been worked.

Tiny Bobbles

Next row (WS) Pick up and p 5 sts evenly along edge of next RS Rectangle.
Rep from * across row—5 WS Rectangles have been worked. Turn.

****Work 1 RH Corner Triangle.
Work 1 row of RS Rectangles. Do *not* turn.
Work 1 LH Corner Triangle.
Work 1 row of WS Rectangles.
Rep from ** to desired length, ending with a LH Corner Triangle completed—1 st remains on the needle. Do *not* turn.

stitch

Make Bobble (MB)
Work (k1, p1, k1) in next st to make 3 sts in one.
P3, turn.
Sl 1, k2tog, psso.

■ Cast on 25 sts (a multiple of 5).

BASE TRIANGLES
*Row 1 (WS) P2, turn.
Row 2 (RS) K2, turn.
Row 3 P3, turn.
Row 4 K1, MB, k1, turn.
Row 5 P4, turn.
Row 6 K4, turn.
Row 7 P5, do *not* turn.
Rep from * for 4 more triangles—5 Base Triangles made. Turn.

RH CORNER TRIANGLE
Row 1 (RS) K2, turn.
Row 2 P2, turn.
Row 3 Inc in first st by knitting into front and back of st, ssk, turn.

Row 4 P3, turn.
Row 5 Inc in first st, MB, ssk, turn.
Row 6 P4, turn.
Row 7 Inc in first st, k2, ssk, do *not* turn.
The RH Corner Triangle is complete. Leave 5 sts on RH needle.

RS RECTANGLES
*Pick-up row (RS) Pick up and k 5 sts evenly along edge of next triangle/rectangle, turn.
Row 1 P5, turn.
Row 2 K4, ssk (with last st of rectangle and first st of next triangle/rectangle), turn.
Row 3 P5, turn.
Row 4 K2, MB, k1, ssk, turn.
Row 5 P5, turn.
Row 6 K4, ssk, turn.
Row 7 P5, turn.
Row 8 K4, ssk, turn.
Row 9 P5, turn.
Row 10 K4, ssk, do *not* turn.
Rep from * across row—4 RS Rectangles have been worked.

LH CORNER TRIANGLE
Pick-up row (RS) Pick up and k 5 sts along edge of last triangle/rectangle, turn.
Row 1 P2tog, p3, turn.
Row 2 K4, turn.
Row 3 P2tog, p2, turn.
Row 4 K1, MB, k1, turn.
Row 5 P2tog, p1, turn.
Row 6 K2, turn.
Row 7 P2tog, do *not* turn—1 st remains on needle.

WS RECTANGLES
Pick-up row (WS) Pick up and p 4 sts evenly along edge of triangle just worked—5 sts, turn.
*Row 1 K5, turn.
Row 2 P4, p2tog (with last st of rectangle and first st of next triangle/rectangle), turn.
Row 3 K5.
Row 4 P4, p2tog, turn.
Row 5 K2, MB, k2, turn.
Row 6 P4, p2tog, turn.
Row 7 K5, turn.
Row 8 P4, p2tog, turn.
Row 9 K5, turn.
Row 10 P4 p2tog, do *not* turn.

END TRIANGLES
*Pick-up row (WS) Pick up and p 4 sts evenly along edge of triangle just worked—5 sts. Turn.
Row 1 (RS) K5, turn.
Row 2 P2tog, p2, p2tog, turn.
Row 3 K4, turn.
Row 4 P2tog, p1, p2tog, turn.
Row 5 K1, MB, k1, turn.
Row 6 P2tog, p2tog, turn.
Row 7 K2, turn.
Row 8 P2tog, p2tog, pass 1st st over 2nd st—1 st remains on needle. Do *not* turn.
Rep from * across row, picking up sts along edge of rectangle instead of triangle.
Fasten off rem st. ❖

Alternating Bobbles

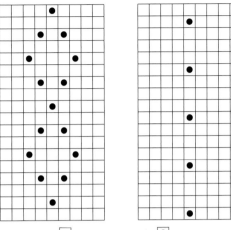

CHART A (RS RECTANGLE) **CHART B (WS RECTANGLE)**

Stitch Key ☐ K on RS, p on WS ⬛ Make Bobble (MB)

stitch

Make Bobble (MB)
In next st work (k1, yo, k1, yo, k1)—5 sts made in 1 st, turn.
P5, turn.
K5, turn.
P2tog, p1, p2tog, turn.
Sl, k2tog, psso—1 st on needle.

■ Cast on 27 sts (multiple of 9 sts).

BASE TRIANGLES
*Row 1 (WS) P2, turn.
Row 2 (RS) K2, turn.
Row 3 P3, turn.
Row 4 K3, turn.
Row 5 P4, turn.
Row 6 K4, turn.
Row 7 P5, turn.
Row 8 K5, turn.
Row 9 P6, turn.
Row 10 K6, turn.
Row 11 P7, turn.
Row 12 K3, MB, k3, turn.
Row 13 P8, turn.
Row 14 K8.

Row 15 P9, do *not* turn.
Rep from * for 2 more triangles—3 Base Triangles made. Turn.

RH CORNER TRIANGLE
Row 1 (RS) K2, turn.
Row 2 P2, turn.
Row 3 Inc in first st by knitting into front and back of st, ssk, turn.
Row 4 P3, turn.
Row 5 Inc in first st, k1, ssk, turn.
Row 6 P4, turn.
Row 7 Inc in first st, k2, ssk, turn.
Row 8 P5, turn.
Row 9 Inc in first st, k3, ssk, turn.
Row 10 P6, turn.
Row 11 Inc in first st, k1, MB, k2, ssk, turn.
Row 12 P7, turn.
Row 13 Inc in first st, k5, ssk.
Row 14 P8, turn.
Row 15 Inc in first st, k6, ssk, do *not* turn.
RH Corner Triangle is complete. Leave 9 sts on RH needle.

RS RECTANGLES
*Pick-up row (RS) Pick up and k 9 sts evenly along edge of next triangle/rectangle, turn.
Work Chart A as foll:
Row 1 (WS) P9, turn.
Row 2 K4, MB, k3, ssk (with last st of chart and first st of next triangle/rectangle), turn.
Row 3 P9, turn.
Rows 4–18 Cont to work RS Rectangle, following Chart A for placement of bobbles. Do *not* turn at end of last row.
Rep from * across row—2 RS Rectangles have been worked.

LH CORNER TRIANGLE
Work LH Corner Triangle same as for Stockinette Stitch sample (page 19), picking up 9 sts (instead of 8) and working bobble on row 4 as foll: K3, MB, k3.

WS RECTANGLES
Pick-up row (WS) Pick up and p 8 sts evenly along edge of triangle just worked—9 sts, turn.
*Row 1 K4, MB, k4, turn.
Row 2 P8, p2tog (with last st of rectangle and first st of next triangle/rectangle), turn.

Row 3 K9, turn.
Row 4 P8, p2tog.
Rows 5–18 Cont to work WS Rectangle following Chart B for placement of bobbles. Do *not* turn at end of last row.
Next row (WS) Pick up and p 9 sts evenly along edge of next RS Rectangle.
Rep from * across row—3 WS Rectangles have been worked. Turn.

**Work 1 RH Corner Triangle.
Work 1 row of RS Rectangles. Do *not* turn.
Work 1 LH Corner Triangle.
Work 1 row of WS Rectangles.
Rep from ** to desired length, ending with a LH Corner Triangle completed—1 st remains on the needle. Do *not* turn.

END TRIANGLES
Work 3 End Triangles same as for Stockinette Stitch sample, picking up 8 sts (instead of 7) and working bobble on row 5 as foll: K3, MB, k3. ❖

Vine Leaf Bobbles

■ Cast on 24 sts
(multiple of 12 sts).

stitches

BPC Sl 1 st to cn and hold to *back*, k1, p1 from cn.
FPC Sl 1 st to cn and hold to *front*, p1, k1 from cn.
Make Bobble (MB)
In next st work (k1, yo, k1, yo, k1)—5 sts made in 1 st, turn.
P5, turn.
K5, turn.
P2tog, p1, p2tog, turn.
Sl, k2tog, psso—1 st on needle.

BASE TRIANGLES

Work 2 Base Triangles same as for Stockinette Stitch sample (page 19), working 12 sts for each triangle (instead of 8).

RH CORNER TRIANGLE

Work RH Corner Triangle same as for Stockinette Stitch sample, working 12 sts (instead of 8).

RS RECTANGLES

*Pick-up row (RS) Pick up and k 12 sts evenly along edge of next triangle/rectangle, turn.
Row 1 (WS) K4, p3, k5, turn.
Row 2 P5, k3, p3, p2tog (with last st of rectangle and first st of next triangle/rectangle), turn.
Row 3 K4, p3, k5, turn.
Row 4 P4, BPC, k1, FPC, p2, p2tog, turn.
Row 5 K3, [p1, k1] 2 times, p1, k4, turn.
Row 6 P3, BPC, p1, k1, p1, FPC, p1, p2tog, turn.
Row 7 K2, [p1, k2] 2 times, p1, k3, turn.
Row 8 P3, MB, p2, k1, p2, MB, p1, p2tog, turn.
Row 9 [K2, p1] 3 times, k3, turn.
Row 10 P6, MB, p4, p2tog, turn.
Rows 11–20 Rep rows 1-10 once.
Row 21 K12, turn.
Row 22 P11, p2tog.
Row 23 and 24 Rep rows 21 and 22. Do *not* turn at end of last row.
Rep from * across row—1 RS Rectangle has been worked.

LH CORNER TRIANGLE

Work LH Corner Triangle same as for Stockinette Stitch sample, working 12 sts (instead of 8).

WS RECTANGLES

Pick-up row (WS) Pick up and p 11 sts evenly along edge of triangle just worked—12 sts, turn.
*Row 1 P4, k3, p5, turn.
Row 2 K5, p3, k3, ssk (with last st of rectangle and first st of next triangle/rectangle), turn.
Row 3 P3, BPC, k1, FPC, p4, turn.
Row 4 K4, [p1, k1] 2 times, p1, k2, ssk, turn.
Row 5 P2, BPC, p1, k1, p1, FPC, p3, turn.
Row 6 K3, [p1, k2] 2 times, p1, k1, ssk, turn.
Row 7 P2, MB, p2, k1, p2, MB, p3, turn.
Row 8 K3, [p1, k2] 2 times, p1, k1, ssk, turn.
Row 9 P5, MB, p6, turn.
Row 10 K5, p3, k3, ssk, turn.
Rows 11–19 Rep rows 1-9.
Rows 20 and 22 K11, ssk, turn.
Rows 21 and 23 P12, turn.
Row 24 K11, ssk, do *not* turn.
Next row (WS) Pick up and p 12 sts evenly along edge of next RS Rectangle.
Rep from * across row—2 WS Rectangles have been worked. Turn.

**Work 1 RH Corner Triangle.
Work 1 row of RS Rectangles.
Do *not* turn.
Work 1 LH Corner Triangle.
Work 1 row of WS Rectangles.
Rep from ** to desired length, ending with a LH Corner Triangle completed—1 st remains on the needle. Do *not* turn.

END TRIANGLES

Work 2 End Triangles same as for Stockinette Stitch sample, picking up 11 sts (instead of 7) and working 2 triangles (instead of 3). ❖

Relief

Cluster Stitch

CLUSTER STITCH

■ K3 and sl these sts to a separate needle. Wind the yarn counter clockwise around the 3 sts 3 times, return the 3 sts to RH needle.

■ Cast on 24 sts (a multiple of 8).

BASE TRIANGLES

Work 3 Base Triangles same as for Stockinette Stitch sample (page 19).

RH CORNER TRIANGLE

Work RH Corner Triangle same as for Stockinette Stitch sample.

RS RECTANGLES

*Pick-up row (RS) Pick up and k 8 sts evenly along edge of next triangle/rectangle, turn.
Row 1 (WS) P8, turn.
Row 2 K3, work cluster st over next 3 sts, k1, ssk (with last st of rectangle and first st of next triangle/rectangle), turn.
Row 3 P8, turn.
Row 4 K7, ssk, turn.
Rows 5–16 Rep rows 1–4 three times. Do *not* turn at end of last row.
Rep from * across row—2 RS Rectangles have been worked.

LH CORNER TRIANGLE

Work LH Corner Triangle same as for Stockinette Stitch sample.

WS RECTANGLES

Pick-up row (WS) Pick up and p 7 sts evenly along edge of triangle just worked, turn.
*Row 1 (RS) K2, work cluster st over next 3 sts, k3, turn.
Row 2 P7, p2tog (with last st of rectangle and first st of next triangle/rectangle), turn.
Row 3 K8, turn.
Row 4 Rep row 2, turn.
Rows 5–16 Rep rows 1–4 three times. Do *not* turn at end of last row.
Next row (WS) Pick up and p 8 sts evenly along edge of next RS Rectangle.
Rep from * across row—3 WS Rectangles have been worked. Turn.

**Work 1 RH Corner Triangle.
Work 1 row of RS Rectangles. Do *not* turn.
Work 1 LH Corner Triangle.
Work 1 row of WS Rectangles.
Rep from ** to desired length, ending with a LH Corner Triangle completed—1 st remains on the needle. Do *not* turn.

END TRIANGLES

Work 3 End Triangles same as for Stockinette Stitch sample. ❖

Relief

Bow Knot

■ BOW KNOT

Slip RH needle under 5 strands made, k next st pulling a long loop through under the strands.

■ Cast on 24 sts (a multiple of 8).

BASE TRIANGLES

*Row 1 (WS) P2, turn.
Row 2 (RS) P2, turn.
Rows 3 and 4 P3, turn.
Rows 5 and 6 P4, turn.
Rows 7 and 8 P5, turn.
Rows 9 and 10 P6, turn.
Rows 11 and 12 P7, turn.
Row 13 P8, do *not* turn.
Rep from * for 2 more triangles—3 Base Triangles made. Turn.

RH CORNER TRIANGLE

Work RH Corner Triangle same as for Stockinette Stitch sample (page 19).

RS RECTANGLES

*Pick-up row (RS) Pick up and k 8 sts evenly along edge of next

---

entre nous

For a neat edge when picking up stitches in the RS Rectangles, pick up into the "bump" of the knit stitch.

---

triangle/rectangle, turn.

Row 1 P8, turn.
Row 2 K7, ssk (with last st of rectangle and first st of next triangle/rectangle), turn.
Row 3 P2, bring yarn to back, sl 3 sts purlwise, bring yarn to front, p3, turn.
Row 4 K7, ssk, turn.
Rows 5–10 Rep last 2 rows 3 times more, turn.
Row 11 Rep row 3.
Row 12 K4, make bow knot, k2, ssk, turn.
Rows 13 and 15 P8, turn.
Rows 14 and 16 K7, ssk, turn.
Do *not* turn at end of last row.

Rep from * across row—2 RS Rectangles have been worked.

LH CORNER TRIANGLE

Work LH Corner Triangle same as for Stockinette Stitch sample.

WS RECTANGLES

Pick-up row (WS) Pick up and p 7 sts evenly along edge of triangle just worked, turn.
*Row 1 (RS) P8, turn.
Row 2 P7, p2tog (with last st of rectangle and first st of next triangle/rectangle), turn.
Rows 3–16 Rep rows 1 and 2 seven times. Do *not* turn.
Next row (WS) Pick up and p 8 sts evenly along edge of next RS Rectangle.
Rep from * across row—3 WS Rectangles have been worked. Turn.

**Work 1 RH Corner Triangle.
Work 1 row of RS Rectangles.
Do *not* turn.

Work 1 LH Corner Triangle.
Work 1 row of WS Rectangles.
Rep from ** to desired length, ending with a LH Corner Triangle completed—1 st remains on the needle. Do *not* turn.

END TRIANGLES

*Pick-up row (WS) Pick up and p 7 sts evenly along edge of triangle just worked. Turn.
Row 1 (RS) P8, turn.
Row 2 P2tog, p5, p2tog, turn.
Row 3 P7, turn.
Row 4 P2tog, p4, p2tog, turn.
Row 5 P6, turn.
Row 6 P2tog, p3, p2tog, turn.
Row 7 P5, turn.
Row 8 P2tog, p2, p2tog, turn.
Row 9 P4, turn.
Row 10 P2tog, p1, p2tog, turn.
Row 11 P3, turn.
Row 12 P2tog, p2tog, turn.
Row 13 P2, turn.
Row 14 P2tog, p2tog, pass 1st st over 2nd st—1 st remains on needle.
Rep from * across row, picking up sts along edge of rectangle instead of triangle.
Fasten off rem st. ❖

Bells

note

The bell stitch starts from an independent base of cast-on stitches. The shape is built in over several rows before it is completed. In this case, certain pattern rows will contain more stitches than the original cast-on, but these extra stitches are gradually reduced to the original number.

■ Cast on 24 sts (a multiple of 8).

BASE TRIANGLES

Work 3 Base Triangles same as for Stockinette Stitch sample (page 19).

RH CORNER TRIANGLE

Work RH Corner Triangle same as for Stockinette Stitch sample.

RS RECTANGLES

*Pick-up row (RS) Pick up and k 8 sts evenly along edge of next triangle/rectangle, turn.
Row 1 (WS) K8, turn.
Row 2 K4, turn, cast on 8 sts, turn, k3, ssk (with last st of rectangle and first st of next triangle/rectangle), turn.

Row 3 K4, p8, k4, turn.
Row 4 K15, ssk, turn.
Row 5 Rep row 3.
Row 6 K4, ssk, k4, k2tog, k3, ssk, turn.
Row 7 K4, p6, k4, turn.
Row 8 K4, ssk, k2, k2tog, k3, ssk, turn.
Row 9 K4, p4, k4, turn.
Row 10 K4, ssk, k2tog, k3, ssk, turn.
Row 11 K4, p2, k4, turn.
Row 12 K4, SKP, k3, ssk, turn.
Row 13 K4, p1, k4, turn.
Row 14 K3, k2tog, k3, ssk, turn.
Row 15 K8, turn.
Row 16 K7, ssk, do *not* turn.
Rep from * across row—2 RS Rectangles have been worked.

LH CORNER TRIANGLE

Work LH Corner Triangle same as for Stockinette Stitch sample.

WS RECTANGLES

Work 3 WS Rectangles same as for Stockinette Stitch sample.
**Work 1 RH Corner Triangle.
Work 1 row of RS Rectangles. Do *not* turn.
Work 1 LH Corner Triangle.
Work 1 row of WS Rectangles.
Rep from ** to desired length, ending with a LH Corner Triangle completed—1 st remains on the needle. Do *not* turn.

END TRIANGLES

Work 3 End Triangles same as for Stockinette Stitch sample. ❖

Two-Color Stockinette

■ **COLOR KEY**
Color A Red
Color B White

■ Cast on 30 sts
(a multiple of 10).

BASE TRIANGLES
Work 3 Base Triangles same as
for Stockinette Stitch sample
(page 19), using A and working
10 sts (instead of 8).

RH CORNER TRIANGLE
Work RH Corner Triangle same as
for Stockinette Stitch sample,
using B and working 10 sts
(instead of 8).

RS RECTANGLES
Work 2 RS Rectangles same as
for Stockinette Stitch sample,
using B and picking up 10 sts
(instead of 8).

LH CORNER TRIANGLE
Work LH Corner Triangle same as
for Stockinette Stitch sample,
using B and working 10 sts
(instead of 8).

WS RECTANGLES
Work 3 WS Rectangles same as
for Stockinette Stitch sample,
using A and picking up 9 sts
(instead of 7)—10 sts on needle.

**Work 1 RH Corner Triangle.
Work 1 row of RS Rectangles. Do
not turn.
Work 1 LH Corner Triangle.
Work 1 row of WS Rectangles.
Rep from ** to desired length,
ending with a LH Corner Triangle
completed—1 st remains on the
needle. Do *not* turn.

END TRIANGLES
Work 3 End Triangles same as for
Stockinette Stitch sample, using
A and picking up 9 sts (instead of
7)—10 sts on needle. ❖

Two-Color Chevrons

■ Cast on 24 sts using A
(a multiple of 4).

BASE TRIANGLES
Work 6 Base Triangles same as for
Stockinette Stitch sample
(page 19), using A and working 4
sts (instead of 8).

RH CORNER TRIANGLE
Work RH Corner Triangle same as
for Stockinette Stitch sample,
working 4 sts (instead of 8) and
following diagram for color
placement.

RS RECTANGLES
Work 5 RS Rectangles same as for
Stockinette Stitch sample, picking
up 4 sts (instead of 8) and following
diagram for color placement.

LH CORNER TRIANGLE
Work LH Corner Triangle same

as for Stockinette Stitch sample,
working 4 sts (instead of 8),
following diagram for color
placement and working last p2tog
in the color of the next rectangle
to be worked.

WS RECTANGLES
Work 6 WS Rectangles same as
for Stockinette Stitch sample,
picking up 3 sts (instead of 7) and
following diagram for color
placement—4 sts on needle.

**Work 1 RH Corner Triangle.
Work 1 row of RS Rectangles.
Do *not* turn.
Work 1 LH Corner Triangle.
Work 1 row of WS Rectangles.
Rep from ** to desired length,
ending with a LH Corner
Triangle completed—1 st
remains on the needle.
Do *not* turn.

Geometrics

Garter-Stitch Diamonds

note

If the first WS Rectangle is a different color than the LH Corner Triangle, work the last p2tog of the triangle in the color to be used for the first WS Rectangle.

■ Cast on 8 sts A, 16 sts B, 8 sts A for a total of 32 sts (a multiple of 32).

BASE TRIANGLES

Work 4 Base Triangles same as for Garter Stitch sample (page 20), matching colors from cast-on row.

RH CORNER TRIANGLE

Work RH Corner Triangle same as for Garter Stitch sample, following diagram for color placement.

RS RECTANGLES

Work 3 RS Rectangles same as for Garter Stitch sample, following diagram for color placement.

LH CORNER TRIANGLE

Work LH Corner Triangle same as for Garter Stitch sample, following diagram for color placement.

WS RECTANGLES

Work 4 WS Rectangles same as for Garter Stitch sample, following diagram for color placement.

**Work 1 RH Corner Triangle. Work 1 row of RS Rectangles. Do *not* turn. Work 1 LH Corner Triangle. Work 1 row of WS Rectangles. Rep from ** to desired length, ending with a LH Corner Triangle completed—1 st remains on the needle. Do *not* turn.

END TRIANGLES

Work 4 End Triangles same as for Garter Stitch sample, following diagram for color placement. ❖

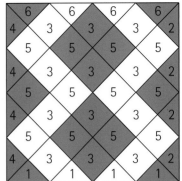

Placement Key

Color Key		Placement Key	
■	Red (A)	1 Base Triangle	4 LH Corner Triangle
□	White (B)	2 RH Corner Triangle	5 WS Rectangle
		3 RS Rectangle	6 End Triangle

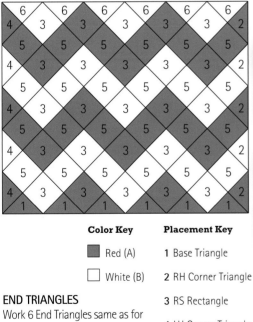

Color Key		Placement Key
■	Red (A)	1 Base Triangle
□	White (B)	2 RH Corner Triangle
		3 RS Rectangle
		4 LH Corner Triangle
		5 WS Rectangle
		6 End Triangle

END TRIANGLES

Work 6 End Triangles same as for Stockinette Stitch sample, picking up 3 sts (instead of 7) and following diagram for color placement—4 sts on needle. ❖

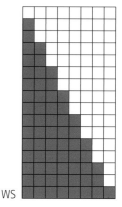

CHART A (RS RECTANGLE)

WS

CHART B (WS RECTANGLE)

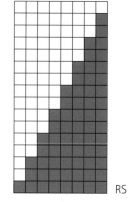

RS

Red & White Triangles

■ Cast on 24 sts with A (a multiple of 8).

BASE TRIANGLES
Work 3 Base Triangles same as for Stockinette Stitch sample (page 19), using A.

RH CORNER TRIANGLE
Work RH Corner Triangle same as for Stockinette Stitch sample, using A.

RS RECTANGLES
*Pick-up row (RS) With B, pick up and k 8 sts evenly along edge of next triangle/rectangle, turn.
Row 1 P8 B, turn.
Row 2 K1 A, k6 B, ssk with B (with last st of rectangle and first st of next triangle/rectangle), turn.
Row 3 P7 B, p1 A, turn.
Row 4 K2 A, k5 B, ssk with B.
Row 5 P6 B, p2 A.
Cont in this way, following chart A through row 16.

Rep from * across row—2 RS Rectangles have been worked.

LH CORNER TRIANGLE
Work LH Corner Triangle as per Stockinette sample, using A and working last p2tog in the color of the next rectangle to be worked.

WS RECTANGLES
Pick-up row (WS) With B, pick up and p 7 sts evenly along edge of triangle just worked, turn.
*Row 1 K8 B, turn.
Row 2 P1 A, p6 B, spp with B (with last st of rectangle and first st of next triangle/rectangle), turn.
Row 3 K7 B, k1 A, turn.
Row 4 P2 A, p5 B, spp with B.
Row 5 K6 B, k2 A, turn.
Cont in this way, following chart B through row 16. Do not turn.
Next row (WS) With B, pick up and p 8 sts evenly along edge of next RS Rectangle.
Rep from * across row—3 WS

Rectangles have been worked. Turn.

**Work 1 RH Corner Triangle.
Work 1 row of RS Rectangles.
Do not turn.
Work 1 LH Corner Triangle.
Work 1 row of WS Rectangles.
Rep from ** to desired length, ending with a LH Corner Triangle completed—1 st remains on the needle. Do not turn.

END TRIANGLES
Work 3 End Triangles same as for Stockinette sample, using B. ❖

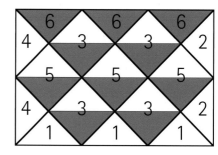

Color Key
☐ White (A)   ■ Red (B)

Placement Key

1 Base Triangle

2 RH Corner Triangle

3 RS Rectangle

4 LH Corner Triangle

5 WS Rectangle

6 End Triangle

Geometrics

Two-Color Basketweave (large)

note

When there are 2 colors shown in 1 rectangle, work half the number of rows in the designated color.

■ Cast on 24 sts using A (a multiple of 8).

BASE TRIANGLES

Work 3 Base Triangles same as for Stockinette Stitch sample (page 19), using A.

RH CORNER TRIANGLE

Work RH Corner Triangle same as for Stockinette Stitch sample, using B.

RS RECTANGLES

Work 2 RS Rectangles same as for Stockinette Stitch sample, following diagram for color placement.

LH CORNER TRIANGLE

Work LH Corner Triangle same as for Stockinette Stitch sample, using B and working last p2tog in the color of the next rectangle to be worked.

WS RECTANGLES

Work 3 WS Rectangles same as for Stockinette Stitch sample, following diagram for color placement.

**Work 1 RH Corner Triangle. Work 1 row of RS Rectangles. Do *not* turn. Work 1 LH Corner Triangle. Work 1 row of WS Rectangles. Rep from ** to desired length, ending with a LH Corner Triangle completed—1 st remains on the needle. Do *not* turn.

END TRIANGLES

Work 3 End Triangles same as for Stockinette Stitch sample, using A. ❖

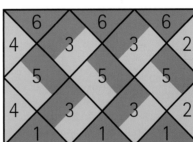

Color Key

■ Dark aqua (A)
□ Light aqua (B)

Placement Key

1 Base Triangle

2 RH Corner Triangle

3 RS Rectangle

4 LH Corner Triangle

5 WS Rectangle

6 End Triangle

entre nous

Twist yarns on WS to prevent holes in work and use a separate bobbin for each block of color.

Geometrics

Two-Color Basketweave (small)

Geometrics

note

When there are 2 colors shown in 1 rectangle, work half the number of sts and/or rows in the designated color.

■ Cast on 24 sts using A (a multiple of 8).

BASE TRIANGLES

Work 3 Base Triangles same as for Stockinette Stitch sample (page 19).

RH CORNER TRIANGLE

Work RH Corner Triangle same as for Stockinette Stitch sample, using B.

RS RECTANGLES

Work 2 RS Rectangles same as for Stockinette Stitch sample, following chart for color placement.

LH CORNER TRIANGLE

Work LH Corner Triangle same as for Stockinette Stitch sample, using B and working last p2tog in the color of the next rectangle to be worked.

WS RECTANGLES

Work 3 WS Rectangles same as for Stockinette Stitch sample, following chart for color placement.

**Work 1 RH Corner Triangle.
Work 1 row of RS Rectangles.
Do *not* turn.
Work 1 LH Corner Triangle.
Work 1 row of WS Rectangles.
Rep from ** to desired length, ending with a LH Corner Triangle completed—1 st remains on the needle. Do *not* turn.

END TRIANGLES

Work 3 End Triangles same as for Stockinette Stitch sample, using A. ❖

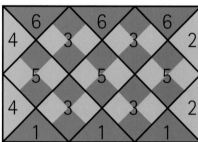

Color Key

■ Dark aqua (A)

□ Light aqua (B)

Placement Key

1 Base Triangle

2 RH Corner Triangle

3 RS Rectangle

4 LH Corner Triangle

5 WS Rectangle

6 End Triangle

entre nous

Twist yarns on WS to prevent holes in work and use a separate bobbin for each block of color.

Patchwork Quilt

note

When there are 2 colors shown in 1 rectangle, you work half the number of sts or rows in the designated color.

■ Cast on 8 sts A, 16 sts B, 8 sts A, for a total of 32 sts (a multiple of 8).

BASE TRIANGLES

Work 4 Base Triangles same as for Stockinette Stitch sample (page 19), matching colors.

RH CORNER TRIANGLE

Work RH Corner Triangle same as for Stockinette Stitch sample, following diagram for color placement.

RS RECTANGLES

Work 3 RS Rectangles same as for Stockinette Stitch sample, following diagram for color placement.

LH CORNER TRIANGLE

Work LH Corner Triangle same as for Stockinette Stitch sample, following diagram for color placement and working last p2tog in the color of the next rectangle to be worked.

WS RECTANGLES

Work 4 WS Rectangles same as for Stockinette Stitch sample, following diagram for color placement.

**Work 1 RH Corner Triangle. Work 1 row of RS Rectangles. Do *not* turn.

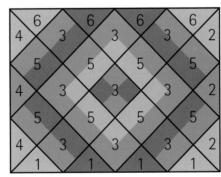

Work 1 LH Corner Triangle. Work 1 row of WS Rectangles. Rep from ** to desired length, ending with a LH Corner Triangle completed—1 st remains on the needle. Do *not* turn.

END TRIANGLES

Work 4 End Triangles same as for Stockinette Stitch sample, following diagram for color placement. ❖

Color Key

□ Lilac (A)
■ Purple (B)
□ Turquoise (C)

Placement Key

1 Base Triangle
2 RH Corner Triangle
3 RS Rectangle
4 LH Corner Triangle
5 WS Rectangle
6 End Triangle

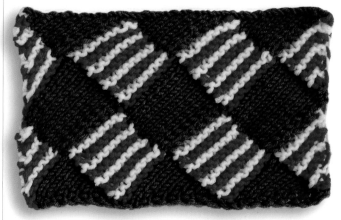

Two-Color Garter Stripes

■ **COLOR KEY**
Color A Red
Color B White

■ **STRIPE PATTERN**
Worked in either knit garter stitch or purl garter stitch as indicated.
Rows 1 and 2 Knit (or purl) with A.
Rows 3 and 4 Knit (or purl) with B.
Rep rows 1–4 for stripe pat.
NOTE When working stripe pat, work 2 rows each color, except for the last row.

■ Cast on 24 sts with A (a multiple of 8).

BASE TRIANGLES
Work 3 Base Triangles same as for Garter Stitch sample (page 20) in purl (instead of knit) garter st, working in stripe pat and carrying color not in use along the last row so that is it ready to begin the next triangle.

RH CORNER TRIANGLE
Beg with A, work RH Corner Triangle same as for Garter Stitch sample, working in stripe pat.

RS RECTANGLES
Work 2 RS Rectangles same as for Garter Stitch sample, continuing in stripe pat.

LH CORNER TRIANGLE
Work LH Corner Triangle same as for Garter Stitch sample, continuing in stripe pat.

WS RECTANGLES
Work 3 WS Rectangles same as for Garter Stitch sample, continuing in stripe pat.

**Work 1 RH Corner Triangle.
Work 1 row of RS Rectangles.
Do *not* turn.
Work 1 LH Corner Triangle.
Work 1 row of WS Rectangles.
Rep from ** to desired length, ending with a LH Corner Triangle completed—1 st remains on the needle. Do *not* turn.

END TRIANGLES
Work 3 End Triangles same as for Garter Stitch sample, continuing in stripe pat. ❖

Red, White and Blue

■ **COLOR KEY**
Color A Blue **Color B** Red
Color C White

STRIPE PATTERN
Rows 1 and 2 Knit with B.
Rows 3 and 4 Knit with C.
Rep rows 1–4 for stripe pat.
NOTE When working stripe pat, work 2 rows each color, except for the last row. Alternate colors for the next triangle or rectangle.

■ Cast on 24 sts with A (a multiple of 8).

BASE TRIANGLES
Work 3 Base Triangles same as for Stockinette Stitch sample (page 19), using A.

RH CORNER TRIANGLE
Beg with B, work RH Corner Triangle same as for Garter Stitch sample (page 20), working in stripe pat. On the last RS row, carry yarn not in use across the row to have the correct color to pick up sts on the next row.

RS RECTANGLES
Work 2 RS Rectangles same as for Garter Stitch sample, continuing in stripe pat.

LH CORNER TRIANGLE
Work LH Corner Triangle same as for Garter Stitch sample, continuing in stripe pat, working the last p2tog with A.

WS RECTANGLES
Work 3 WS Rectangles same as for Stockinette Stitch sample, using A.

**Work 1 RH Corner Triangle.
Work 1 row of RS Rectangles.
Do *not* turn.
Work 1 LH Corner Triangle.
Work 1 row of WS Rectangles.
Rep from ** to desired length, ending with a LH Corner Triangle completed—1 st remains on the needle. Do *not* turn.

END TRIANGLES
Work 3 End Triangles same as for Stockinette Stitch sample, using A. ❖

Two-Color Alternating Stripes & Solids

■ **COLOR KEY**
Color A White
Color B Dark Gray

■ **STRIPE PATTERN**
Rows 1 and 2 Knit with B.
Rows 3 and 4 Knit with A.
Rep rows 1–4 for stripe pat.

■ Cast on 24 sts with A
(multiple of 8).

BASE TRIANGLES
Work 3 Base Triangles same
as for Garter Stitch sample
(page 20) with A.

RH CORNER TRIANGLE
Work RH Corner Triangle same as
for Garter Stitch sample, working
in stripe pat and carrying A
across the last row.
NOTE Carry A along back of
work, weaving in every 2 sts so
that yarn is at the correct
position for the next rectangle.

RS RECTANGLES
Work 2 RS Rectangles same as
for Garter Stitch sample, working
in stripe pat and beg with A.
NOTE On the last row, carry yarn
not in use loosely along back of

work, weaving in every 2 sts so
that yarn is at the correct
position for the next rectangle.

LH CORNER TRIANGLE
Work LH Corner Triangle same as
for Garter Stitch sample, working
in stripe pat and beg with A.

WS RECTANGLES
Work 3 WS Rectangles same as
for Garter Stitch sample with A.

****Work 1 RH Corner Triangle.
Work 1 row of RS Rectangles.
Do *not* turn.**

Work 1 LH Corner Triangle.
Work 1 row of WS Rectangles.
Rep from ** to desired length,
ending with a LH Corner Triangle
completed—1 st remains on the
needle. Do *not* turn.

END TRIANGLES
Work 3 End Triangles same as for
Garter Stitch sample with A. ❖

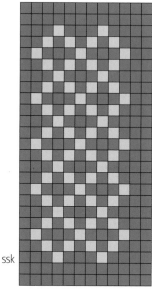

ssk

pick-up
row

Fair Isle Diamonds

■ Cast on 24 sts
(a multiple of 12).

BASE TRIANGLES

Work 2 Base Triangles same as
for Stockinette Stitch sample
(page 19), using Main Color (MC)
and working 12 sts (instead of 8).

RH CORNER TRIANGLE

Work RH Corner Triangle same as
for Stockinette sample, using MC
and working 12 sts (instead of 8).

RS RECTANGLES

Work 1 RS Rectangle same
as for Stockinette Stitch sample,
following Chart A and picking
up 12 sts (instead of 8).

LH CORNER TRIANGLE

Work LH Corner Triangle same
as for Stockinette Stitch sample,
using MC and working 12 sts
(instead of 8).

WS RECTANGLES

Work 2 WS Rectangles same as
for Stockinette Stitch sample,
following Chart B and picking up
11 sts (instead of 7)—12 sts on
needle.

**Work 1 RH Corner Triangle.
Work 1 row of RS Rectangles.
Do not turn.
Work 1 LH Corner Triangle.
Work 1 row of WS Rectangles.
Rep from ** to desired length,

ending with a LH Corner Triangle
completed—1 st remains on the
needle. Do not turn.

END TRIANGLES

Work 2 End Triangles same as for
Stockinette Stitch sample, using
MC and picking up 11 sts (instead
of 7)—12 sts on needle. ❖

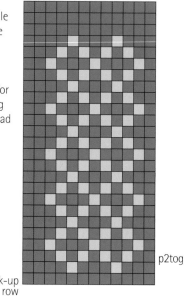

p2tog

pick-up
row

Color Key

■ Purple (MC)

□ Light turquoise

■ Dark turquoise

Colorwork

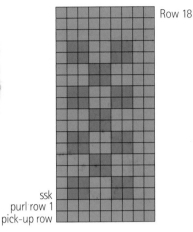

CHART A (RS RECTANGLE)

Row 18

ssk
purl row 1
pick-up row

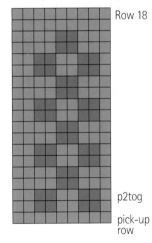

CHART B (WS RECTANGLE)

Row 18

p2tog

pick-up
row

Fair Isle Checks

■ Cast on 18 sts (a multiple of 9).

BASE TRIANGLES
Work 2 Base Triangles same as for Stockinette Stitch sample (page 19), using Main Color (MC) and working 9 sts (instead of 8).

RH CORNER TRIANGLE
Work RH Corner Triangle same as for Stockinette Stitch sample, using Main Color and working 9 sts (instead of 8).

RS RECTANGLES
Work 1 RS Rectangle same as for Stockinette Stitch sample, following Chart A and picking up 9 sts (instead of 8).

LH CORNER TRIANGLE
Work LH Corner Triangle same as for Stockinette Stitch sample, using MC and working 9 sts (instead of 8).

WS RECTANGLES
Work 2 WS Rectangles same as for Stockinette Stitch sample, following Chart B and picking up 8 sts (instead of 7)—9 sts on needle.

**Work 1 RH Corner Triangle. Work 1 row of RS Rectangles. Do *not* turn.
Work 1 LH Corner Triangle. Work 1 row of WS Rectangles. Rep from ** to desired length, ending with a LH Corner Triangle completed—1 st remains on the needle. Do *not* turn.

END TRIANGLES
Work 2 End Triangles same as for Stockinette Stitch sample, using MC and picking up 8 sts (instead of 7)—9 sts on needle. ❖

Color Key

■ Lavender (MC)

■ Turquoise

■ Purple

Hearts

- Cast on 16 sts (a multiple of 8).

BASE TRIANGLES
Work 2 Base Triangles same as for Stockinette Stitch sample (page 19), using Main Color (MC).

RH CORNER TRIANGLE
Work RH Corner Triangle same as for Stockinette Stitch sample, using MC.

RS RECTANGLES
Work 1 RS Rectangle same as for Stockinette Stitch sample, following Chart A.

LH CORNER TRIANGLE
Work LH Corner Triangle same as for Stockinette Stitch sample, using MC.

WS RECTANGLES
Work 2 WS Rectangles same as for Stockinette Stitch sample, following Chart B.

**Work 1 RH Corner Triangle.
Work 1 row of RS Rectangles.
Do *not* turn.
Work 1 LH Corner Triangle.
Work 1 row of WS Rectangles.
Rep from ** to desired length, ending with a LH Corner Triangle completed—1 st remains on the needle. Do *not* turn.

END TRIANGLES
Work 2 End Triangles same as for Stockinette Stitch sample, using MC. ❖

CHART A (RS RECTANGLE)

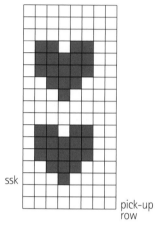

ssk

pick-up row

CHART B (WS RECTANGLE)

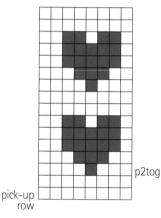

pick-up row

p2tog

Color Key

- ⬛ Red
- ⬜ White (MC)

Two-Color Zigzag

- **COLOR KEY**
Color A White Color B Light Gray
Color C Dark Gray

NOTE When changing colors, twist yarns on WS to prevent holes in work. Carry colors not in use *loosely* across back of work.

- Cast on 24 sts with A (multiple of 8)

BASE TRIANGLES
Work 3 Base Triangles same as for Garter Stitch sample (page 19) with A.

RH CORNER TRIANGLE
Work RH Corner Triangle same as for Garter Stitch sample with A.

Two-Color Dots

- **COLOR KEY**
Color A Light Gray
Color B Dark Gray

NOTE When changing colors, twist yarns on WS to prevent holes in work. Carry colors not in use *loosely* across back of work.

- Cast on 24 sts with A (multiple of 8).

BASE TRIANGLES
Work 3 Base Triangles same as for Stockinette Stitch sample (page 19) with A.

RH CORNER TRIANGLE
Work RH Corner Triangle same as for Stockinette Stitch sample with B.

Colorwork

RS RECTANGLES

*Pick-up row (RS) With A, pick up and k 8 sts evenly along edge of next triangle/rectangle, turn.
Row 1 With A, k8, turn.
Row 2 K2 A, join B and k4, k1 A, with A ssk (with last st of rectangle and first st of next triangle/rectangle), turn.
Row 3 K2 A, p4 B, k2 A, turn.
Rep last 2 rows until 2 A sts rem on LH needle.
Row 15 K8 A, turn.
Row 16 K7 A, ssk, do *not* turn.
Rep from * across row—2 RS Rectangles have been worked.

LH CORNER TRIANGLE
Work RH Corner Triangle same as for Garter Stitch sample with A.

WS RECTANGLES
Pick-up row (WS) With A, pick up and p 7 sts evenly along edge of triangle just worked, turn.
*Row 1 P8 A, turn.
Row 2 P2 A, join C and p4, p1 A, with A spp (with last st of rectangle and first st of next triangle/rectangle), turn.
Row 3 P2 A, k4 C, p2 A, turn.
Rep last 2 rows until 2 A sts rem on LH needle.
Row 15 P8 A, turn.
Row 16 P7A, ssp, do *not* turn.
Next row (WS) With A, pick up and p 8 sts evenly along edge of next RS Rectangle.
Rep from * across row—3 WS Rectangles have been worked. Turn.

****Work 1 RH Corner Triangle.
Work 1 row of RS Rectangles.
Do *not* turn.
Work 1 LH Corner Triangle.

Work 1 row of WS Rectangles. Rep from ** to desired length, ending with a LH Corner Triangle completed—1 st remains on the needle. Do *not* turn.

END TRIANGLES
Work 3 End Triangles same as for Garter Stitch sample with A. ❖

RS RECTANGLES

*Pick-up row (RS) With A, pick up and k 8 sts evenly along edge of next triangle/rectangle, turn.
Row 1 (WS) With A, p8, turn.
Row 2 K3 A, join B and k2 B, k2 A, with A ssk (with last st of rectangle and first st of next triangle/rectangle), turn.
Row 3 P3 A, p2 B, p3 A, turn.
Row 4 K7 A, with A ssk, turn.
Row 5 Rep row 1.
Rows 6–16 Rep rows 2–5 twice, then rows 2–4 once more. Do *not* turn at end of last row.
Rep from * across row—2 RS Rectangles have been worked.

LH CORNER TRIANGLE
Work LH Corner Triangle same as for Stockinette Stitch sample with B. **NOTE** The last p2tog is worked in A.

WS RECTANGLES
Pick up row (WS) With A, Pick up and p 7 sts evenly along edge of triangle just worked, turn.
*Row 1 K3 A, k2 B, k3 A turn.
Row 2 P3 A, p2 B, p2 A, with A spp (with last st of rectangle and first st of next triangle/rectangle), turn.
Row 3 With A, k8, turn.
Row 4 With A, p7, spp, turn.
Rows 5–16 Rep rows 1–4 three times. Do *not* turn at end of last row.
Next row (WS) Pick up and p 8 sts evenly along edge of next RS Rectangle.
Rep from * across row—3 WS Rectangles have been worked. Turn.

****Work 1 RH Corner Triangle.
Work 1 row of RS Rectangles.

Do *not* turn.
Work 1 LH Corner Triangle.
Work 1 row of WS Rectangles.
Rep from ** to desired length, ending with a LH Corner Triangle completed—1 st remains on

the needle. Do *not* turn.

END TRIANGLES
Work 3 End Triangles same as for Stockinette Stitch sample with A. ❖

Colorwork

Felted & Striped Garter Stitch

■ **COLOR KEY**
A Lavender **B** Aqua

■ **STRIPE PATTERN**
Rows 1 and 2 K with B
Rows 3 and 4 K with A
Rep rows 1–4 for stripe pat.

NOTE Use needles that are three times larger than the suggested needle size for the given yarn.

■ Cast on 24 sts with A
(a multiple of 8).

BASE TRIANGLES
Work 3 Base Triangles same as for Garter Stitch sample (page 20) with A.

RH CORNER TRIANGLE
Work RH Corner Triangle same as for Garter Stitch sample, working in stripe pat and carrying A across the last row.
NOTE Carry A along back of work, weaving in every 2 sts so that yarn is at the correct position for the next rectangle.

RS RECTANGLES
Work 2 RS Rectangles same as for Garter Stitch sample, working in stripe pat and beg with A.
NOTE On the last row, carry yarn not in use loosely along back of work, weaving in every 2 sts so that yarn is at the correct position for the next rectangle.

LH CORNER TRIANGLE
Work LH Corner Triangle same as for Garter Stitch sample, working in stripe pat and beg with A.

WS RECTANGLES
Work 3 WS Rectangles same as for Garter Stitch sample with A.

**Work 1 RH Corner Triangle.
Work 1 row of RS Rectangles.
Do *not* turn.
Work 1 LH Corner Triangle.
Work 1 row of WS Rectangles.
Rep from ** to desired length, ending with a LH Corner Triangle completed—1 st remains on the needle. Do *not* turn.

END TRIANGLES
Work 3 End Triangles same as for Garter Stitch sample with A.

FINISHING
To felt swatch, place in washing machine set to hot wash/cold rinse with low water level.
Add a pair of jeans for abrasion and balanced agitation.
Add 1 tablespoon dishwashing detergent and ¼ cup baking soda at beginning of wash cycle.
Repeat cycle, if necessary, until swatch is felted to desired size.
Let air dry and block piece flat. ❖

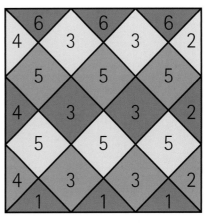

Color Key

■ Dark blue

■ Medium blue

□ Light blue

Placement Key

1 Base Triangle

2 RH Corner Triangle

3 RS Rectangle

4 LH Corner Triangle

5 WS Rectangle

6 End Triangle

entre nous

Test yarns to be felted for colorfastness before beginning a project.

Felted Shades of Blue

note

Use needles that are three times larger than the suggested needle size for the given yarn.

■ Cast on 24 sts using A (a multiple of 8).

BASE TRIANGLES

Work 3 Base Triangles same as for Stockinette Stitch sample (page 19), following diagram for color placement.

RH CORNER TRIANGLE

Work RH Corner Triangle same as for Stockinette Stitch sample, following diagram for color placement.

RS RECTANGLES

Work 2 RS Rectangles same as for Stockinette Stitch sample, following diagram for color placement.

LH CORNER TRIANGLE

Work LH Corner Triangle same as for Stockinette Stitch sample, following diagram for color placement and working last p2tog in the color of the next rectangle to be worked.

WS RECTANGLES

Work 3 WS Rectangles same as for Stockinette Stitch sample, following diagram for color placement.

**Work 1 RH Corner Triangle.
Work 1 row of RS Rectangles.
Do *not* turn.
Work 1 LH Corner Triangle.
Work 1 row of WS Rectangles.
Rep from ** to desired length, ending with a LH Corner Triangle completed—1 st remains on the needle. Do *not* turn.

END TRIANGLES

Work 3 End Triangles same as for Stockinette Stitch sample, following diagram for color placement.

FINISHING

To felt swatch, place in washing machine set to hot wash/cold rinse with low water level. Add a pair of jeans for abrasion and balanced agitation. Add 1 tablespoon dishwashing detergent and ¼ cup baking soda at beginning of wash cycle. Rep cycle, if necessary, until swatch is felted to desired size. Let air dry and block piece flat. ❖

Mélanges

Two-Color Garter Stripes

■ **COLOR KEY**
Color A 1 strand blue multi
Color B 2 strands fine mohair

■ **STRIPE PATTERN**
Rows 1 and 2 Knit with A.
Rows 3 and 4 Knit with B.
Rep rows 1–4 for stripe pat.
NOTE When working stripe pat,
work 2 rows each color, except
for the last row.

■ Cast on 24 sts with Color A
(a multiple of 8).

BASE TRIANGLES
Work 3 Base Triangles same as
for Garter Stitch sample (page
20), working in stripe pat.
NOTE Wrong side of stripe will
show on right side of work.

RH CORNER TRIANGLE
Beg with A, work RH Corner
Triangle same as for Garter Stitch
sample, working in stripe pat.

RS RECTANGLES
Work 2 RS Rectangles same

as for Garter Stitch sample,
continuing in stripe pat.

LH CORNER TRIANGLE
Work LH Corner Triangle same
as for Garter Stitch sample,
continuing in stripe pat.

WS RECTANGLES
Work 3 WS Rectangles, working
pick-up row in purl and the
rectangle in knit garter st same
as for Garter Stitch sample,
continuing in stripe pat.

**Work 1 RH Corner Triangle.
Work 1 row of RS Rectangles. Do
not turn.
Work 1 LH Corner Triangle.
Work 1 row of WS Rectangles.
Rep from ** to desired length,
ending with a LH Corner Triangle
completed—1 st remains on the
needle. Do *not* turn.

END TRIANGLES
Work 3 End Triangles same as for
Garter Stitch sample, continuing
in stripe pat. ❖

Two-Yarn Stockinette

■ **COLOR KEY**
A 2 strands blue multi
B 2 strands fine mohair

■ Cast on 24 sts (a multiple of 8).

BASE TRIANGLES
Work 3 Base Triangles same as
for Stockinette Stitch sample
(page 19), using 2 strands of A.

RH CORNER TRIANGLE
Work RH Corner Triangle same
as for Stockinette Stitch sample,
using 2 strands of B.

RS RECTANGLES
Work 2 RS Rectangles same
as for Stockinette Stitch sample,
using 2 strands of B.

LH CORNER TRIANGLE
Work LH Corner Triangle same
as for Stockinette Stitch sample,
using 2 strands of B.

WS RECTANGLES
Work 3 WS Rectangles same as
for Stockinette Stitch sample,

using 2 strands of A.

**Work 1 RH Corner Triangle.
Work 1 row of RS Rectangles.
Do *not* turn.
Work 1 LH Corner Triangle.
Work 1 row of WS Rectangles.
Rep from ** to desired length,
ending with a LH Corner Triangle
completed—1 st remains on the
needle. Do *not* turn.

END TRIANGLES
Work 3 End Triangles same as for
Stockinette Stitch sample, using
2 strands of A. ❖

Mélanges

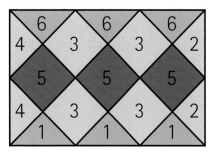

Placement Key

1 Base Triangle

2 RH Corner Triangle

3 RS Rectangle

4 LH Corner Triangle

5 WS Rectangle

6 End Triangle

Color Key

⬜ Lilac – St st (A)

⬜ Turquoise – seed st (B)

⬛ Lavender – St st (C)

Stockinette & Seed St in 3 Colors

■ SEED STITCH

Row 1 *K1, p1; rep from * to end.

Row 2 K the purl sts and p the knit sts.

Rep row 2 for seed st.

■ Cast on 18 sts with A (a multiple of 6).

BASE TRIANGLES

Work 3 Base Triangles same as for Stockinette Stitch sample (page 19), using A and working 6 sts (instead of 8).

RH CORNER TRIANGLE

Join B.

Row 1 (RS) P1, k1, turn.

Row 2 (WS) K1, p1, turn.

Row 3 Inc in first st by (k1, p1) in next st, ssk, turn.

Row 4 Work 3 sts in seed st, turn.

Row 5 Inc in first st by (p1, k1) in next st, p1, ssk, turn.

Row 6 Work 4 sts in seed st, turn.

Row 7 Inc in first st by (k1, p1) in next st, k1, p1, ssk, turn.

Row 8 Work 5 sts in seed st, turn.

Row 9 Inc in first st by (p1, k1) in next st, p1, k1, p1, ssk, do *not* turn.

The RH Corner Triangle is complete. Leave 6 sts on RH needle.

RS RECTANGLES

*Pick-up row (RS) With B, pick up and k 6 sts evenly along edge of next triangle/rectangle, turn.

Row 1 (WS) [K1, p1] 3 times, turn.

Row 2 [P1, k1] 2 times, p1, ssk (with last st of rectangle and first st of next triangle/rectangle), turn.

Rows 3–12 Rep rows 1 and 2 five times.

Rep from * across row—2 RS Rectangles have been worked.

LH CORNER TRIANGLE

Pick-up row (RS) Pick up and k 6 sts along edge of last triangle/rectangle, turn.

Row 1 (WS) P2tog, work 4 sts in seed st, turn.

Row 2 Work 5 sts in seed st, turn.

Row 3 K2tog, work 3 sts in seed st, turn.

Row 4 Work 4 sts in seed st, turn.

Row 5 P2tog, work 2 sts in seed st, turn.

Row 6 Work 3 sts in seed st, turn.

Row 7 K2tog, work 1 st in seed st, turn.

Row 8 Work 2 sts in seed st, turn.

Row 9 P2tog with C, do *not* turn—1 st remains on needle.

WS RECTANGLES

Work 3 WS Rectangles same as for Stockinette Stitch sample, using C and picking up 5 sts (instead of 7)—6 sts on needle.

**Work 1 RH Corner Triangle. Work 1 row of RS Rectangles. Do *not* turn.

Work 1 LH Corner Triangle. Work 1 row of WS Rectangles. Rep from ** to desired length, ending with a LH Corner Triangle completed—1 st remains on the needle. Do *not* turn.

END TRIANGLES

Work 3 End Triangles same as for Stockinette Stitch sample, using A and picking up 5 sts (instead of 7)—6 sts on needle. ❖

entre nous

Try working the WS Rectangles in another yarn, such as silk, for an interesting effect.

Stockinette & Double Seed Stitch With Ribbon Yarn

■ This swatch uses a rayon ribbon yarn. It is the same pattern as the Stockinette and Double Seed Stitch swatch (page 25) but the finished look is very different due to the yarn. ❖

Stockinette Stitch With Beaded Yarn

NOTE This swatch uses a beaded silk yarn.

■ Cast on 21 sts (a multiple of 7). Work same as for Stockinette Stitch sample (page 19), working with 7 sts (instead of 8) and picking up 6 sts (instead of 7) on the WS Rectangles and End Triangles. ❖

Two-Yarn Stockinette (Large)

■ **COLOR KEY**
A Purple wool
B Purple bouclé mohair with glass beads

■ Cast on 24 sts with A (a multiple of 8).

BASE TRIANGLES
Work 3 Base Triangles same as for Stockinette Stitch sample (page 19), using A.

RH CORNER TRIANGLE
Work RH Corner Triangle same as for Stockinette Stitch sample, using B.

RS RECTANGLES
Work 2 RS Rectangles same as for Stockinette Stitch sample, using B.

LH CORNER TRIANGLE
Work LH Corner Triangle same as for Stockinette Stitch sample, using B.

entre nous

While knitting, some of the beads may fall to the wrong side of the work. After finishing, gently pull the beads to the right side.

WS RECTANGLES
Work 3 WS Rectangles same as for Stockinette Stitch sample, using A.

**Work 1 RH Corner Triangle.
Work 1 row of RS Rectangles.
Do *not* turn.
Work 1 LH Corner Triangle.
Work 1 row of WS Rectangles.
Rep from ** to desired length, ending with a LH Corner Triangle completed—1 st remains on the needle. Do *not* turn.

END TRIANGLES
Work 3 End Triangles same as for Stockinette Stitch sample, using A. ❖

Two-Yarn Stockinette (Small)

NOTE These small triangles and rectangles give a more delicate appearance than those of the larger version (opposite page).

■ **COLOR KEY**
A Purple wool **B** Purple bouclé mohair with glass beads

■ Cast on 16 sts with A (a multiple of 4). Work same as larger version (opposite), working 4 sts (instead of 8) for each triangle and rectangle and picking up 3 sts (instead of 7) on the WS Rectangles and End Triangles. ❖

Stockinette Stitch With Beads

NOTE This swatch uses a multi-colored mohair-blend yarn. The beads are attached after knitting.

■ Cast on 30 sts (a multiple of 10). Work same as for Stockinette Stitch sample (page 19), working with 10 sts (instead of 8) and picking up 9 sts (instead of 7) on the WS Rectangles and End Triangles.

ATTACHING BEADS
Sew one bead at each intersection (see photo). ❖

Stockinette Stitch With Multicolored Yarn

■ This swatch uses a multicolored yarn. The appearance of the color changes will vary depending on the number of stitches and rows used. The directions for the swatch shown are the same as for the Stockinette Stitch sample (page 19). ❖

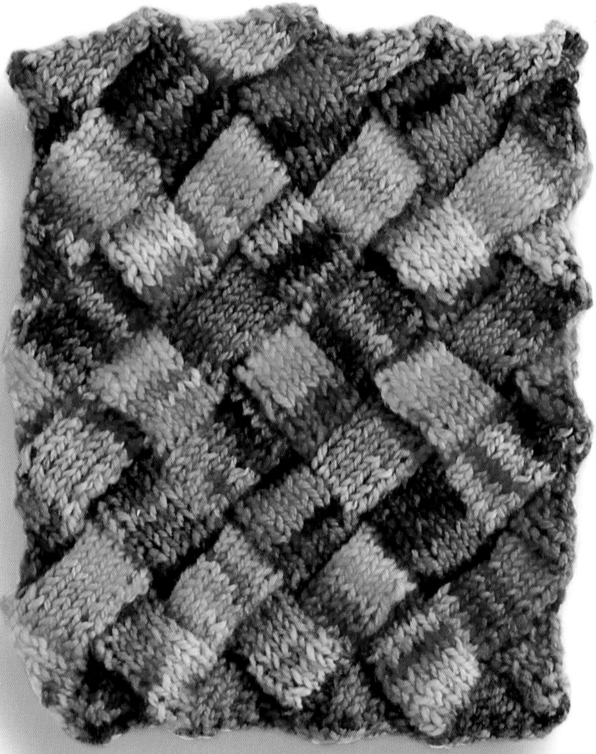

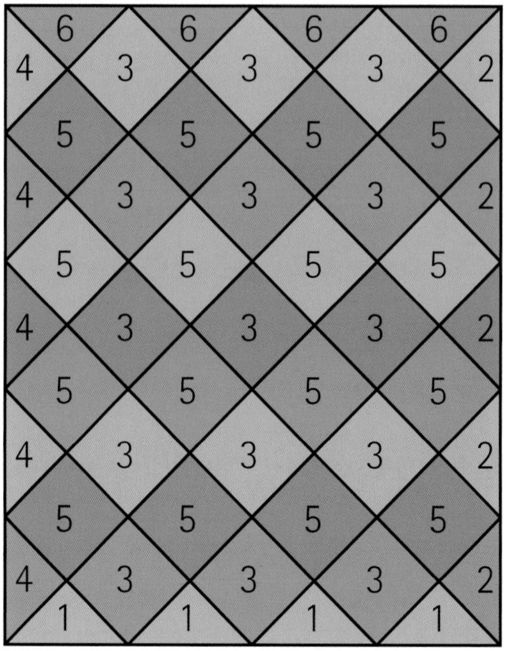
6 6 6 6
4 3 3 3 2
5 5 5 5
4 3 3 3 2
5 5 5 5
4 3 3 3 2
5 5 5 5
4 3 3 3 2
5 5 5 5
4 3 3 3 2
1 1 1 1

Stash Buster

■ **COLOR KEY**
A Blue multi
B Purple multi
C Red-orange multi

> **note**
> This swatch was made with three multicolored yarns. You can use any number of colors, choosing odds and ends from your yarn stash in any color combination.

■ Cast on 24 sts with A (a multiple of 6).

BASE TRIANGLES
Work 4 Base Triangles same as for Stockinette Stitch sample (page 19), using A and working 6 sts (instead of 8).

RH CORNER TRIANGLE
Work RH Corner Triangle same as for Stockinette Stitch sample, using B.

RS RECTANGLES
Work 3 RS Rectangles same as for Stockinette sample, using B.

LH CORNER TRIANGLE
Work LH Corner Triangle same as for Stockinette sample, using B.

WS RECTANGLES
Work 4 WS Rectangles as per Stockinette sample, using C.

NOTE Cont to alternate colors A, B and C following diagram, or change colors are desired.

**Work 1 RH Corner Triangle.
Work 1 row of RS Rectangles.
Do *not* turn.
Work 1 LH Corner Triangle.
Work 1 row of WS Rectangles.
Rep from ** to desired length, ending with a LH Corner Triangle completed—1 st remains on the needle. Do *not* turn.

END TRIANGLES
Work 4 End Triangles same as for Stockinette Stitch sample, using B and picking up 5 sts (instead of 7). ❖

Color Key

- Blue multi (A)
- Purple multi (B)
- Red-orange multi (C)

Placement Key

1 Base Triangle
2 RH Corner Triangle
3 RS Rectangle
4 LH Corner Triangle
5 WS Rectangle
6 End Triangle

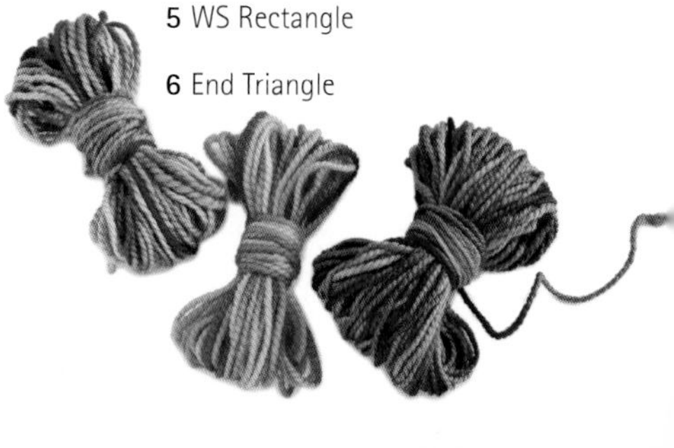

Ridge Stitch in Self-Striping Yarn

■ **RIDGE STITCH ON RS**
Row 1 (RS) Knit.
Row 2 Purl.
Ridge Row 3 Purl.
Row 4 Purl.
Rep rows 1–4 for ridge st on RS.

■ Cast on 24 sts (a multiple of 8).

BASE TRIANGLES
Work 3 Base Triangles same as for Stockinette Stitch sample (page 19).

RH CORNER TRIANGLE
Work RH Corner Triangle same as for Stockinette Stitch sample.

RS RECTANGLES
*Pick-up row (RS)** Pick up and k 8 sts evenly along edge of next triangle/rectangle, turn.
Row 1 (WS) P8, turn (row 2 of ridge pat).
Row 2 P7 (ridge row 3 of ridge pat), spp (with last st of rectangle and first st of next triangle/rectangle), turn.
Row 3 P8, turn (row 4 of ridge pat).
Row 4 K7 (row 1 of ridge pat), skp, turn.

Rows 5–16 Rep rows 1 and 4 three times. Do *not* turn at end of last row.
NOTE On the knit (RS) rows, work skp and on the purl (RS) rows, work spp.
Rep from * across row—2 RS Rectangles have been worked.

LH CORNER TRIANGLE
Work LH Corner Triangle same as for Stockinette Stitch sample.

WS RECTANGLES
Work 3 WS Rectangles same as for Stockinette Stitch sample.

**Work 1 RH Corner Triangle.
Work 1 row of RS Rectangles.
Do *not* turn.
Work 1 LH Corner Triangle.
Work 1 row of WS Rectangles.
Rep from ** to desired length, ending with a LH Corner Triangle completed—1 st remains on the needle. Do *not* turn.

END TRIANGLES
Work 3 End Triangles same as for Stockinette Stitch sample. ❖

Stockinette With Multicolored and Textured Yarn

■ This swatch uses a multicolored and multitextured yarn. The appearance of the color changes will vary depending on the number of stitches and rows used. The yarn is produced in such a way that it gives a patchwork effect to the sample. The directions are the same as for the Stockinette Stitch sample (page 19). ❖

Mélanges

Tiny Ribbon Buds

NOTE For embroidery you will need 5yd/5m 4mm ribbon from Mokuba in light purple (A), dark purple (B) and green (C).

■ Cast on 24 sts (a multiple of 4).

BASE TRIANGLES
Work 6 Base Triangles same as for Stockinette Stitch sample (p. 19), using 4 sts (instead of 8).

RH CORNER TRIANGLE
Work RH Corner Triangle same as for Stockinette Stitch sample, using 4 sts (instead of 8).

RS RECTANGLES
Work 5 RS Rectangles same as for Stockinette Stitch sample, picking up 4 sts (instead of 8).

LH CORNER TRIANGLE
Work LH Corner Triangle same as for Stockinette Stitch sample, working 4 sts (instead of 8).

WS RECTANGLES
Work 6 WS Rectangles same as for Stockinette Stitch sample, picking up 3 sts (instead of 7).

**Work 1 RH Corner Triangle. Work 1 row of RS Rectangles. Do *not* turn. Work 1 LH Corner Triangle. Work 1 row of WS Rectangles. Rep from ** to desired length, ending with a LH Corner Triangle—1 st remains on the needle. Do *not* turn.

END TRIANGLES
Work 6 End Triangles same as for Stockinette Stitch sample, picking up 3 sts (instead of 7).

FINISHING
For flowers, work 2 bullion sts in A and 2 lazy daisy sts in B (see page 102). Work stems in fern st with C. See photo for placement. ❖

FERN STITCH

Bullion Roses

NOTE For embroidery, you will need 1 skein each of DMC *Perle Cotton #5* in light purple (A), dark purple (B) and green (C).

■ Cast on 18 sts (a multiple of 6).

BASE TRIANGLES
Work 3 Base Triangles same as for Stockinette Stitch sample (page 19), using 6 sts (instead of 8).

RH CORNER TRIANGLE
Work RH Corner Triangle same as for Stockinette Stitch, using 6 sts (instead of 8).

RS RECTANGLES
Work 2 RS Rectangles same as for Stockinette Stitch, picking up 6 sts (instead of 8).

LH CORNER TRIANGLE
Work LH Corner Triangle same as for Stockinette Stitch, working 6 sts (instead of 8).

WS RECTANGLES
Work 3 WS Rectangles same as for Stockinette Stitch, picking up 5 sts (instead of 7).

**Work 1 RH Corner Triangle. Work 1 row of RS Rectangles. Do *not* turn. Work 1 LH Corner Triangle. Work 1 row of WS Rectangles. Rep from ** to desired length, ending with a LH Corner Triangle completed—1 st remains on the needle. Do *not* turn.

END TRIANGLES
Work 3 End Triangles same as for Stockinette Stitch, picking up 5 sts (instead of 7).

FINISHING
Embroider flowers and stems in center of RS Rectangles as foll: With A, work 2 bullion sts (see page 102) with 8 wraps each. With B, work outside petals in bullion st. With C, work two lazy daisy st leaves (see page 102). ❖

Garter Stripes & Daisies

■ COLOR KEY
A Blue
B Green

■ STRIPE PATTERN
Rows 1 and 2 Knit with B.
Rows 3 and 4 Knit with A.
Rep rows 1–4 for stripe pat.

NOTES
1 When working stripe pat, work 2 rows each color, except for the last row.
2 For embroidery, you will need 1 skein of DMC *Perle Cotton #5* in #369 pale green.

■ Cast on 24 sts with A (a multiple of 8).

BASE TRIANGLES
Work 3 Base Triangles same as for Stockinette Stitch sample (page 19), using A.

RH CORNER TRIANGLE
Beg with B, work RH Corner Triangle same as for Garter Stitch sample (page 20), working in stripe pat.

NOTE On the last RS row, carrying yarn not in use across the row to have the correct color to pick up sts on the next row.

RS RECTANGLES
Work 2 RS Rectangles same as for Garter Stitch sample, continuing in stripe pat.

LH CORNER TRIANGLE
Work LH Corner Triangle same as for Garter Stitch sample, continuing in stripe pat.

WS RECTANGLES
Work 3 WS Rectangles same as for Stockinette Stitch sample, using B.

**Work 1 RH Corner Triangle.
Work 1 row of RS Rectangles. Do *not* turn.
Work 1 LH Corner Triangle.
Work 1 row of WS Rectangles.
Rep from ****** to desired length, ending with a LH Corner Triangle completed—1 st remains on the needle. Do *not* turn.

END TRIANGLES
Work 3 End Triangles same as for Stockinette Stitch sample, using A.

FINISHING
Using embroidery thread, work lazy daisy st flowers (see page 102) in center of each St st rectangle. Using A, work French knot in center of each flower. ❖

FRENCH KNOT

Two-Color Stockinette With Daisies

NOTE You will need 5 yd/5m of 4mm ribbon from Mokuba in light yellow and 1 skein DMC *Perle Cotton #5* in pale yellow.

■ **COLOR KEY**
A Olive green   **B** Bright green

■ Cast on 18 sts with A (a multiple of 6).

BASE TRIANGLES
Work 3 Base Triangles as per Stockinette sample (page 19), using A and working 6 sts for each triangle (instead of 8).

RH CORNER TRIANGLE
Work RH Corner Triangle as per Stockinette sample, using B and working 6 sts (instead of 8).

RS RECTANGLES
Work 2 RS Rectangle as per Stockinette sample, using B and picking up 6 sts (instead of 8).

LH CORNER TRIANGLE
Work LH Corner Triangle same as for Stockinette Stitch sample, using B, picking up 5 sts (instead of 8) and working last p2tog in the color of the next rectangle to be worked.

WS RECTANGLES
Work 3 WS Rectangles as per Stockinette sample using A and picking up 5 sts (instead of 7)—6 sts on needle.
**Work 1 RH Corner Triangle. Work 1 row of RS Rectangles. Do *not* turn. Work 1 LH Corner Triangle. Work 1 row of WS Rectangles. Rep from ** to desired length, ending with a LH Corner Triangle completed—1 st remains on the needle. Do *not* turn.

END TRIANGLES
Work 3 End Triangles as per Stockinette sample, using A and picking up 5 sts (instead of 7).

FINISHING
With ribbon, embroider lazy daisy st flowers (page 102) at each intersection. With 2 strands of embroidery thread, work French knot (page 71) in center of each flower. ❖

Ribbon Roses

NOTE For embroidery, you need 5 yd/5m of 4mm ribbon from Mokuba in pink (A) and green (B).

■ Cast on 24 sts (multiple of 6). Work as per Stockinette sample (page 19), using 6 sts (instead of 8), making 4 each Base Triangles and End Triangles (instead of 3) and picking up 5 sts (instead of 7) on the WS Rectangles and End Triangles.

SPIDER WEB STITCH

FINISHING
With A, work a rose over each intersection, using spider web stitch with 5 "spokes." With B, work the lazy daisy st leaves (see page 102). ❖

Embroidery

Crazy Quilt

NOTE You will need one skein of DMC *Perle Cotton #5* in color #729 gold for embroidery

■ Cast on 8 sts A, 8 sts B, 8 sts C, 8 sts D, for a total of 32 sts (a multiple of 8).

BASE TRIANGLES
Work 4 Base Triangles same as for Stockinette Stitch sample (page 19), matching colors.

RH CORNER TRIANGLE
Work RH Corner Triangle same as for Stockinette Stitch sample, following diagram for color.

RS RECTANGLES
Work 3 RS Rectangles same as for Stockinette Stitch sample, following diagram for color placement.

LH CORNER TRIANGLE
Work LH Corner Triangle same

as for Stockinette Stitch sample, following diagram for color placement and working last p2tog in the color of the next rectangle to be worked.

WS RECTANGLES
Work 4 WS Rectangles same as for Stockinette Stitch sample, following diagram for color placement.

**Work 1 RH Corner Triangle. Work 1 row of RS Rectangles. Do *not* turn.

Work 1 LH Corner Triangle. Work 1 row of WS Rectangles. Rep from ** to desired length, ending with a LH Corner Triangle completed—1 st remains on the needle. Do *not* turn.

END TRIANGLES
Work 4 End Triangles as per Stockinette sample, following

FEATHER STITCH

Color Key	Placement Key
■ Brown (A)	1 Base Triangle
■ Slate blue (B)	2 RH Corner Triangle
■ Burgundy (C)	3 RS Rectangle
■ Olive green (D)	4 LH Corner Triangle
	5 WS Rectangle
	6 End Triangle

diagram for color placement.

FINISHING
With embroidery thread, outline each triangle/rectangle with feather stitch as in photo. ❖

CHAPTER 3

the patterns

INTERMEDIATE

uptown poncho

An entrelac panel takes center stage on this updated poncho. Knitting just a section in entrelac is an effortless way to incorporate the technique.

SIZE
Sized for adult woman.

FINISHED MEASUREMENTS
Width 32"/81.5cm
Length 22"/56cm

MATERIALS
- 14 1¾oz/50g balls (each approx 92yd/83m) of Tahki Yarns/Tahki•Stacy Charles, Inc. *Lana* (organic merino wool) in #4 slate (4)

- Sizes 10½ and 11 (6.5 and 8mm) circular needles, each 16"/40cm long, for turtleneck

- Size 10½ (6.5mm) circular needle, 36"/92cm long, for side ribs

- One pair size 10 (6mm) needles OR SIZE TO OBTAIN GAUGE

- Stitch holder

GAUGES
- 15 sts and 22 rows = 4"/10cm over St st using size 10 (6mm) needles.

- 22 sts = 8"/20.5cm over entrelac pat using size 10 (6mm) needles. TAKE TIME TO CHECK GAUGES.

ENTRELAC PANEL
With straight needles, cast on 22 sts (multiple of 11 sts).

BASE TRIANGLES
*Row 1 (WS) P2, turn.
Row 2 (RS) K2, turn.
Row 3 P3, turn.
Row 4 K3, turn.
Row 5 P4, turn.
Row 6 K4, turn.
Row 7 P5, turn.
Row 8 K5, turn.
Row 9 P6, turn.
Row 10 K6, turn.
Row 11 P7, turn.
Row 12 K7, turn.
Row 13 P8, turn.
Row 14 K8, turn.
Row 15 P9, turn.
Row 16 K9, turn.
Row 17 P10, turn.
Row 18 K10, turn.
Row 19 P11, do *not* turn.
Rep from * for one more triangle—2 Base Triangles made. Turn.

RH CORNER TRIANGLE
Row 1 (RS) K2, turn.

Row 2 (WS) P2, turn.
Row 3 Inc in first st by knitting into front and back of st, ssk, turn.
Row 4 P3, turn.
Row 5 Inc in first st, k1, ssk, turn.
Row 6 P4, turn.
Row 7 Inc in first st, k2, ssk, turn.
Row 8 P5, turn.
Row 9 Inc in first st, k3, ssk, turn.
Row 10 P6, turn.
Row 11 Inc in first st, k4, ssk, turn.
Row 12 P7, turn.
Row 13 Inc in first st, k5, ssk, turn.
Row 14 P8, turn.
Row 15 Inc in first st, k6, ssk, turn.
Row 16 P9, turn.
Row 17 Inc in first st, k7, ssk, turn.
Row 18 P10, turn.
Row 19 Inc in first st, k8, ssk, do *not* turn.
RH Corner Triangle is completed. Leave 11 sts on RH needle.

RS RECTANGLES
Pick-up row (RS) Pick up and k 11 sts evenly along edge of next triangle/rectangle, turn.

Row 1 (WS) [P2, k2] twice, p3, turn.
Row 2 K3, p2, k2, p2, k1, ssk (with last st of rectangle and first st of next triangle/rectangle), turn.
Rows 3–22 Rep rows 1 and 2 ten times. Do *not* turn at end of last row.

LH CORNER TRIANGLE
Pick-up row (RS) Pick up and k 11 sts along edge of last triangle/rectangle, turn.
Row 1 P2tog, p9, turn.
Row 2 K10, turn.
Row 3 P2tog, p8, turn.
Row 4 K9, turn.
Row 5 P2tog, p7, turn.
Row 6 K8, turn.
Row 7 P2tog, p6, turn.
Row 8 K7, turn.
Row 9 P2tog, p5, turn.
Row 10 K6, turn.
Row 11 P2tog, p4, turn.
Row 12 K5, turn.
Row 13 P2tog, p3, turn.
Row 14 K4, turn.
Row 15 P2tog, p2, turn.
Row 16 K3, turn.

Row 17 P2tog, p1, turn.
Row 18 K2, turn.
Row 19 P2tog, do *not* turn—1 st remains on RH needle.

WS RECTANGLES

Pick-up row (WS) Pick up and p 10 sts evenly along edge of triangle just worked—11 sts on RH needle, turn.
*****Row 1** [K2, p2] twice, k3, turn.
Row 2 P3, k2, p2, k2, p1, p2tog (with last st of rectangle and first st of next triangle/rectangle), turn.
Rows 3–22 Rep rows 1 and 2 ten times. Do *not* turn at end of last row.
Next row (WS) Pick up and p 11 sts evenly along edge of next RS Rectangle, turn.
NOTE Pick up along 3rd st, making k2 sts rem on RS of pat for rib.
Rep from * across row—2 WS Rectangles have been worked. Turn.
Work 1 RH Corner Triangle.
Work 1 RS Rectangle, picking up 11 sts along edge of WS Rectangle and picking up the 3rd st of k3, thus making k2 sts rem on RS of pat for rib.
Rep as for RS Rectangle.
Cont as established until 5 rows

of RS Rectangles are worked. Work 1 LH Triangle. Piece measures approx 20"/50.5cm from beg.

END TRIANGLES

*****Pick-up row (WS)** Pick up and p 10 sts evenly along edge of triangle just worked—11 sts on RH needle. Turn.
Row 1 (RS) K11, turn.
Row 2 P2tog, p8, p2tog, turn.
Row 3 K10, turn.
Row 4 P2tog, p7, p2tog, turn.
Row 5 K9, turn.
Cont as established until next RS row is K2, turn.
Next row (WS) P2tog, p2tog, pass 1st st over 2nd st—1 st remains on RH needle.
Rep from * across row, picking up sts along edge of rectangle instead of triangle.
Fasten off rem st.

BACK

With straight needles, cast on 118 sts. Work in St st for 20"/50.5cm, or same length as Entrelac Panel. Bind off 42 sts at beg of next 2 rows. Leave rem 34 sts on a holder.

FRONT STRIPS (MAKE 2)

With straight needles, cast on 42 sts. Work in St st for 20"/50.5cm. Bind off.

FINISHING

Block pieces to measurements. Sew Entrelac Panel between 2 Front Strips. Sew shoulder seams.

SIDE RIB SECTION

With longer 10½ (6.5mm) circular needle and RS facing, pick up and k 110 sts along side edge.
Next row (WS) P2, *k2, p2; rep from * to end.
Next row (RS) K2, *p2, k2; rep from * to end.
Rep last 2 rows twice more.
Bind off loosely in rib.

LOWER EDGE RIB (BACK)

With longer 10½ (6.5mm) circular needle and RS facing, pick up and k 130 sts along edge, beginning at Side Rib edge. Work in k2, p2 rib as before for 3"/7.5cm. Bind off loosely in rib.

LOWER EDGE RIB (FRONT)

Work as for Back Rib.

TURTLENECK

With shorter 10½ (6.5mm) circular needle and RS facing, pick up and k 72 sts around neck edge, beg at back neck. Work in k2, p2 rib for 4"/10cm. Change to size 11 (8mm) circular needle and cont in rib for 5"/12.5cm more. Bind off loosely in rib. ❖

entre nous

I chose a ribbed stitch for the entrelac panel, but you can substitute one of your favorite pattern stitches, as long as it measures approximately 8"/ 20.5cm wide.

EASY

stitch sampler floor pillows

Simple pillows make a cozy accent for any room and are the perfect canvas to practice incorporating different stitches into an entrelac pattern. Start with stockinette if you're new to entrelac.

FINISHED MEASUREMENTS
Approx 23"/58.5cm square

MATERIALS
■ 7 3½oz/100g skeins (each approx 127yd/115m) of Classic Elite Yarns *Montera* (llama/wool) each in #3829 aqua ice (A), #3817 soft iris (B) and #3857 air Blue (C) (4)

■ One pair size 8 (5mm) needles OR SIZE TO OBTAIN GAUGE

■ Three 24"/61cm square pillow forms

GAUGE
16 sts and 20 rows = 4"/10cm over St st.
TAKE TIME TO CHECK GAUGE

Stockinette Pillow
FRONT
With A, cast on 70 sts (multiple of 10 sts).

BASE TRIANGLES
*Row 1 (WS) P2, turn.
Row 2 (RS) K2, turn.
Row 3 P3, turn.
Row 4 K3, turn.
Row 5 P4, turn.
Row 6 K4, turn.
Row 7 P5, turn.
Row 8 K5, turn.
Row 9 P6, turn.
Row 10 K6, turn.
Row 11 P7, turn.
Row 12 K7, turn.
Row 13 P8, turn.
Row 14 K8, turn.
Row 15 P9, turn.
Row 16 K9, turn.
Row 17 P10, do *not* turn.
Rep from * for 6 more triangles—7 Base Triangles made. Turn.

RH CORNER TRIANGLE
Row 1 (RS) K2, turn.
Row 2 (WS) P2, turn.
Row 3 Inc in first st by knitting into front and back of st, ssk, turn.
Row 4 P3, turn.
Row 5 Inc in first st, k1, ssk, turn.
Row 6 P4, turn.
Row 7 Inc in first st, k2, ssk, turn.
Row 8 P5, turn.
Row 9 Inc in first st, k3, ssk, turn.
Row 10 P6, turn.
Row 11 Inc in first st, k4, ssk, turn.
Row 12 P7, turn.
Row 13 Inc in first st, k5, ssk, turn.
Row 14 P8, turn.
Row 15 Inc in first st, k6, ssk, turn.
Row 16 P9, turn.
Row 17 Inc in first st, k7, ssk, do *not* turn.
The RH Corner Triangle is complete. Leave 10 sts on RH needle.

RS RECTANGLES
*Pick-up row (RS) Pick up and k 10 sts evenly along edge of next triangle/rectangle, turn.
Row 1 (WS) P10, turn.
Row 2 K9, ssk (with last st of rectangle and first st of next triangle/rectangle), turn.
Rows 3–20 Rep rows 1 and 2 nine times. Do *not* turn at end of last row.
Rep from * across row—6 RS Rectangles made.

LH CORNER TRIANGLE
Pick-up row (RS) Pick up and k 10 sts along edge of last triangle/rectangle, turn.
Row 1 P2tog, p8, turn.
Row 2 K9, turn.
Row 3 P2tog, p7, turn.
Row 4 K8, turn.
Row 5 P2tog, p6, turn.
Row 6 K7, turn.
Row 7 P2tog, p5, turn.
Row 8 K6, turn.
Row 9 P2tog, p4, turn.
Row 10 K5, turn.
Row 11 P2tog, p3, turn.
Row 12 K4, turn.
Row 13 P2tog, p2, turn.
Row 14 K3, turn.
Row 15 P2tog, p1, turn.
Row 16 K2, turn.
Row 17 P2tog, do *not* turn—1 st remains on RH needle.

WS RECTANGLES
Pick-up row (WS) Pick up and p 9 sts evenly along edge of triangle just worked—10 sts on RH needle, turn.

Clockwise from above:
Stockinette Pillow,
Ridge Stitch Pillow,
Stockinette and Seed
Stitch Pillow.

*Row 1 K10, turn.
Row 2 P8, p2tog (with last st of rectangle and first st of next triangle/rectangle), turn.
Rows 3–20 Rep rows 1 and 2 nine times. Do *not* turn.
Next row (WS) Pick up and p 10 sts evenly along edge of next RS Rectangle.
Rep from * across row—7 WS Rectangles made. Turn.

Continue as established until 6 rows of RS Rectangles have been worked. End with a LH Corner Triangle made.

Ridge Stitch Pillow

END TRIANGLES
*Pick-up row (WS) Pick up and p 9 sts evenly along edge of triangle just worked—10 sts on RH needle. Turn.
Row 1 (RS) K10, turn.
Row 2 P2tog, p7, p2tog, turn.
Row 3 K9, turn.
Row 4 P2tog, p6, p2tog, turn.
Row 5 K8, turn.
Row 6 P2tog, p5, p2tog, turn.
Row 7 K7, turn.
Row 8 P2tog, p4, p2tog, turn.
Row 9 K6, turn.
Row 10 P2tog, p3, p2tog, turn.
Row 11 K5, turn.
Row 12 P2tog, p2, p2tog, turn.
Row 13 K4, turn.
Row 14 P2tog, p1, p2tog, turn.
Row 15 K3, turn.
Row 16 P2tog, p2tog, turn.
Row 17 K2, turn.
Row 18 P2tog, p2tog, pass first st over 2nd st—1 st rem on RH needle.
Rep from * across row, picking up sts along edge of rectangle instead of triangle.
Fasten off.

BACK
With A, cast on 92 sts. Work in St st for 20"/50.5cm. Bind off.

FLAP
With A, cast on 92 sts. Work in St st for 6"/15.5cm. Bind off.

Ridge Stitch Pillow
FRONT
With B, cast on 70 sts (multiple of 10 sts).

BASE TRIANGLES
Work 7 Base Triangles (10 sts each) as for Stockinette Pillow.

RH CORNER TRIANGLE
Work as for Stockinette Pillow.

RS RECTANGLES
*Pick-up row (RS) Pick up and k 10 sts evenly along edge of next triangle/rectangle, turn.
Rows 1, 3, 5 and 7 (WS) P10, turn.
Row 2 (Ridge) P9, spp (with last st of rectangle and first st of next triangle/rectangle), turn.
Row 4 K10, ssk.
Row 6 P9, spp, turn.
Rep rows 4–7 three times more.
Rep row 1 once more.
Do *not* turn at end of last row.
NOTE On the knit (RS) rows, work skp, and on the purl (RS) rows, work spp.
Rep from * across row—6 RS Rectangles made.

LH CORNER TRIANGLE.
Work same as for Stockinette Pillow.

WS RECTANGLES
Pick-up row (WS) Pick up and p

10 sts evenly along edge of triangle just worked, turn.
*Row 1 (RS) P10, turn.
Row 2 P9, p2tog (with last st of rectangle and first st of next triangle/rectangle), turn.
Row 3 K10, turn.
Row 4 P9, p2tog, turn.
Row 5 P10, turn.
Row 6 Rep row 4.
Rep rows 3–6 three times. Do *not* turn.
Next row (WS) Pick up and p 10 sts evenly along edge of next RS Rectangle.

Rep from * across row—7 WS Rectangles made. Turn.

Cont as established until 6 rows of RS Rectangles have been made, end with LH Corner Triangle made.

END TRIANGLES
Work same as for Stockinette Pillow.

BACK
Work as for Stockinette Pillow using B.

Stockinette & Seed Stitch Pillow

SEED STITCH
Row 1 *K1, p1; rep from * to end.
Row 2 K the purl sts and p the knit sts.
Rep row 2 for seed st.

FRONT
With C, cast on 70 sts (multiple of 10 sts).

BASE TRIANGLES
Work 7 Base Triangles (10 sts each) as for Stockinette Pillow.

RH CORNER TRIANGLE
Work in St st as for Stockinette Pillow. Leave sts on RH needle.

RS RECTANGLES
*Pick-up row (RS) Pick up and k 10 sts evenly along edge of next triangle/rectangle, turn.
Work same as Stockinette Pillow.

LH CORNER TRIANGLE
Pick-up row (RS) Pick up and k 10 sts along edge of last triangle/rectangle, turn.
Work same as Stockinette Pillow.

WS RECTANGLES
Pick-up row (WS) Pick up and p 9 sts evenly along edge of triangle just worked—10 sts, turn.
*Row 1 (RS) [P1, k1] 5 times, turn.
Row 2 [K1, p1] 4 times,

k1, spp (with last st of rectangle and first st of next triangle/rectangle), turn.
Rows 3–20 Rep rows 1 and 2 nine times. Do *not* turn.
Next row (WS) Pick up and p 10 sts evenly along edge of next RS Rectangle.
Rep from * across row—7 WS Rectangles made. Turn.

Continue as established until 6 rows of RS Rectangles have been made, ending with a LH Corner Triangle made.

END TRIANGLES
Work same as for Stockinette Pillow.

BACK
Work as for Stockinette Pillow using C.

**FINISHING
(FOR ALL PILLOWS)**
Block pieces to measurements. Sew larger back piece to front starting at bottom edge. Sew side seams. Sew smaller back piece to front along top edge and overlapping at sides. Insert pillow form, slip-stitch closed. ❖

Stockinette & Seed Stitch Pillow

BEGINNER

silk and cashmere cowl

The structure of this cowl couldn't be simpler, but knitting it in a variegated, luxe yarn upgrades it to a fashionable accessory.

SIZE
Sized for adult woman.

FINISHED MEASUREMENTS
8" x 24"/20.5cm x 61cm

MATERIALS
■ 1 3½oz/100g skein (approx 256yd/234m) of Artyarns, *Ensemble* (silk/cashmere) in #173 multi (3)

■ One pair size 5 (3.75mm) needles OR SIZE TO OBTAIN GAUGE

GAUGES
■ 20 sts and 28 rows = 4"/10cm over St st using size 5 (3.75mm) needles.

■ 3 base triangles = 4"/10cm over St st using size 5 (3.75mm) needles.
TAKE TIME TO CHECK GAUGES.

COWL
Cast on 30 sts (a multiple of 5).

BASE TRIANGLES
*Row 1 (WS) P2, turn.
Row 2 (RS) K2, turn.
Row 3 P3, turn.
Row 4 K3, turn.
Row 5 P4, turn.
Row 6 K4, turn.
Row 7 P5, do *not* turn.
Rep from * for 5 more Base Triangles—6 Base Triangles made. Turn.

RH CORNER TRIANGLE
Row 1 (RS) K2, turn.
Row 2 (WS) P2, turn.
Row 3 Inc in first st by knitting into front and back of st, ssk, turn.
Row 4 P3 turn.
Row 5 Inc in first st, k1, ssk, turn.
Row 6 P4, turn.
Row 7 Inc in first st, k2, ssk, do *not* turn.
The RH Corner Triangle is complete. Leave 5 sts on RH needle.

RS RECTANGLES
*Pick-up row (RS) Pick up and k 5 sts evenly along edge of next triangle/rectangle, turn.
Row 1 (WS) P5, turn.
Row 2 K4, ssk (with last st of rectangle and first st of next triangle/rectangle), turn.
Rows 3–10 Rep rows 1 and 2 four times. Do *not* turn at end of last row.
Rep from * across row—5 RS Rectangles have been worked.

LH CORNER TRIANGLE
Pick-up row (RS) Pick up and k 5 sts along edge of last triangle/rectangle, turn.
Row 1 P2tog, p3, turn.
Row 2 K4, turn.
Row 3 P2tog, p2, turn.
Row 4 K3, turn.
Row 5 P2tog, k1, turn.

WS RECTANGLES
Pick-up row (WS) Pick up and p 4 sts evenly along edge of triangle just worked—5 sts on RH needle, turn.
*Row 1 K5, turn.
Row 2 P4, p2tog (with last st of rectangle and first st of next triangle/rectangle), turn.
Rows 3–10 Rep rows 1 and 2 four times. Do *not* turn.
Next row (WS) Pick up and p 5 sts evenly along edge of next RS Rectangle.
Rep from * across row—6 WS Rectangles have been worked. Turn.
**Work 1 RH Corner Triangle. Work 1 row of RS Rectangles. Do *not* turn.

Work 1 LH Corner Triangle. Work 1 row of WS Rectangles. Rep from ** until 17 rows of RS Rectangles have been made, ending with a LH Corner Triangle made—1 st remains on the RH needle. Do *not* turn.

END TRIANGLES
*Pick-up row (WS) Pick up and p 4 sts evenly along edge of triangle just worked—5 sts on RH needle. Turn.
Row 1 (RS) K5, turn.
Row 2 P2tog, p2, p2tog, turn.
Row 3 K4, turn.
Row 4 P2tog, p1, p2tog, turn.
Row 5 K3, turn.
Row 6 P2tog, p2tog, turn.
Row 7 K2, turn.
Row 8 P2tog, p2tog, pass 1st st over 2nd st—1 st remains on RH needle.
Rep from * across row, picking up sts along edge of rectangles instead of triangle, until 6 End Triangles have been made. Fasten off.

FINISHING
Sew cast-on edge and bound-off edge together to form a circle. ❖

sassy socks

Kick up your heels in Lori Steinberg's socks embellished with beautiful entrelac cuffs. The muted colors give them vintage charm.

SIZE
Women's Small/Medium

FINISHED MEASUREMENTS
Foot circumference 7½"/19cm
Length from top of cuff to bottom of heel 8½"/20.5cm
Length from back of heel to tip of toe 8¾"/22cm

MATERIALS
■ 1 1¾oz/50g hank (approx 185yd/169m) each of Louet *Gems Fingering Weight* (merino wool) in #47 orange (A) and #26 raspberry (C) ❶
■ 2 hanks in #44 brown (B)
■ One set (5) size 1 (2.75mm) double-pointed needles (dpn)
■ Stitch marker

GAUGE
32 sts and 48 rnds = 4"/10cm over St st using size 1 (2.75mm) needles.
TAKE TIME TO CHECK GAUGE.

SOCKS
With A, cast on 60 sts, pm and join, being careful not to twist sts on needles.
Rib rnd P1, *k3, p2; rep from * to last st, p1. Rep last rnd until piece measures 1"/2.5cm from beg.
*K 1 rnd. Rib 1 rnd; rep from * until piece measures 2"/5cm from beg, end with a K rnd. Cut A.

BEG BASE TRIANGLES
*Next rnd (RS)** With B, k2, turn.
Row 2 (WS) Sl 1, p1, turn.
Row 3 Sl 1, k2, turn.
Row 4 and all WS rows Sl 1, p to end, turn.
Row 5 Sl 1, k3, turn.
Row 7 Sl 1, k3, p1, turn.
Row 9 Sl 1, k3, p2, turn.
Row 11 Sl 1, k3, p2, k1, turn.
Row 13 Sl 1, k3, p2, k2, turn.
Row 15 Sl 1, k3, p2, k3, turn.
Row 17 Sl 1, k3, p2, k4, turn.
Row 19 Sl 1, k3, p2, k4, do *not* turn—1 Triangle made.

Rep from * until 6 triangles have been made. Cut B.

BEG RECTANGLES
With RS facing and C, beg at lower corner of first triangle, pick up and k 10 sts along edge of first triangle, turn.
Row 1 (WS) Sl 1, p8, p2 tog with next st on 6th triangle, turn.
Row 2 and all RS rows Sl 1, k9, turn.
Rep rows 1 and 2 until all sts of triangle have been worked.

NEXT RECTANGLE
Pick up and purl 10 sts along edge of 6th triangle, work same as for first rectangle, beg with row 2. Cont to work rectangles until 6 rectangles made. Do *not* turn. Cut C.
With B and WS facing, beg at lower edge of first rectangle, pick up and p 10 sts along edge of this rectangle. Turn.

Next row (RS) Sl 1, k3, p2, k3, ssk with next st from last C rectangle worked. Turn.
Next row (WS) Sl, p9. Rep last 2 rows until all 10 C rectangle sts have been made. Do *not* turn.

NEXT RECTANGLE
*Pick up and k 10 sts along edge of rectangle, turn. Beg with a WS row, work as for previous rectangle. Rep from * until 6 B rectangles have been made. Cut B. With C, pick up and k 10 sts along edge of first B rectangle worked. Work as for previous rnd of C rectangles until 6 C rectangles have been made. Do *not* turn. Cut C.

END TRIANGLES
With WS facing, rejoin B to lower corner of first rectangle worked in previous rnd. Pick up and p 10 sts, turn.
Sl 1, k3, p2, k3, ssk with first st of last rectangle worked, turn.

86

*Next row and all WS rows Sl 1, p to end, turn.
Next row (RS) Sl 1, ssk, turn.
Next row (RS) Sl 1, k1, ssk, turn.
Next row (RS) Sl 1, k2, ssk, turn.
Next row (RS) Sl 1, k3, ssk, turn.
Next row (RS) Sl 1, p1, k3, ssk, turn.
Next row (RS) Sl 1, p2, k3, ssk, turn.
Next row (RS) Sl 1, k1, p2, k3, ssk, turn.
Next row (RS) Sl 1, k2, p2, k3, ssk, turn.
Next row (RS) Sl 1, k3, p2, k3, ssk,* do *not* turn—10 sts.

2ND TRIANGLE

Pick up and k 10 sts, turn.
Rep from * to * as on previous End Triangle.
Next row (WS) Sl 1, p9, turn.
Next row Sl 1, k3, p2, k3, ssk, turn.
Rep 2nd triangle 4 times more.
Pm, k 1 rnd. (**NOTE** To close gaps at beg of each triangle, lift running thread from back to front onto point of LH needle and k2tog with next st.)

BEG HEEL FLAP

Next rnd K15, turn.
Next rnd With A, p30 (heel is worked on the first and last 15 sts of the rnd).
Row 1 [Sl 1, k1] 15 times.
Row 2 Sl 1, p29.
Rep rows 1 and 2 until heel flap measures 2¼"/5.5cm, end with row 1.

TURN HEEL (WS)

Sl 1, p16, p2tog, p1, turn.
Sl 1, k5, ssk, k1, turn.
Sl 1, p6, p2tog, p1, turn.
Cont in this way, working 1 more stitch before the decrease each row until 18 sts rem.

GUSSET

With A, pick up and k 18 sts along edge of heel flap. Cut A. With B, work in pat as established (keeping p2 sections aligned and rem sts in St st) across 30 instep sts. Pick up and k 18 sts along 2nd edge of heel flap, k9 heel sts.
Next rnd Knit around.
Next rnd K to last 3 sts of first needle, k2tog, k1; work in pat across instep sts, on last needle k1, ssk, k to end.
Rep last 2 rnds until 60 sts rem. Cont even in pat until sock measures 7"/17.5cm from back of heel. Cut B.

SHAPE TOE

Dec rnd With A, k to last 3 sts on first needle, k2tog, k1, on instep k1, ssk, k to last 3 instep sts, k2tog, k1, on last needle k1, ssk, k to end of rnd.
Next rnd Knit.
Rep last 2 rnds until 32 sts rem. Rep dec rnd every rnd until 16 sts rem. Place sts evenly on 2 needles and use Kitchener stitch to graft toe sts. ❖

entre nous

If you want to knit knee-length socks instead, work more rows of rectangles. You could even adapt this design to create legwarmers by ending before the heel and repeating the ribbed edging.

Knit the socks in a single hue for an even more subdued effect, or go crazy with bright, contrasting colors.

EASY

market tote

Knit in machine-washable linen yarn, this handy bag makes it easy to just say no to plastic—use it to transport groceries or even yarn!

FINISHED MEASUREMENTS
13"/33cm wide x 15"/38cm tall

MATERIALS
- 2 3½ oz/100g skeins (each approx 270yd/247m) of Louet Euroflax *Fine/Sport Weight* (linen) in #671 seafoam green (2)
- One pair size 5 (3.75mm) needles OR SIZE TO OBTAIN GAUGE
- Two size 5 (3.75mm) double-pointed needles (dpns) for I-cord
- Stitch markers

GAUGE
17 sts and 36 rows = 4"/10cm over garter ridge pattern.
TAKE TIME TO CHECK GAUGE.

stitches

RIDGE STITCH ON RIGHT SIDE
Row 1 (RS) Knit.
Row 2 Purl.
Ridge row 3 Purl.
Row 4 Purl.
Rep rows 1–4 for ridge st on RS.

RIDGE STITCH ON WRONG SIDE
Row 1 (WS) Purl.
Ridge row 2 Purl.
Row 3 Purl.
Row 4 Knit.
Rep rows 1–4 for ridge st on WS.

FRONT
Cast on 50 sts (multiple of 10 sts). Work 6 rows in garter stitch for opening edge of bag. On last row place 4 markers each 10 sts apart for 5 Base Triangles.

BASE TRIANGLES
*Row 1 (WS) P2, turn.
Row 2 (RS) K2, turn.
Row 3 P3, turn.
Row 4 K3, turn.
Row 5 P4, turn.
Row 6 K4, turn.
Row 7 P5, turn.
Row 8 K5, turn.
Row 9 P6, turn.
Row 10 K6, turn.
Row 11 P7, turn.
Row 12 K7, turn.
Row 13 P8, turn.
Row 14 K8, turn.
Row 15 P9, turn.
Row 16 K9, turn.
Row 17 P10, do *not* turn.
Rep from * for 4 more Base Triangles—5 Base Triangles made. Turn.

RH CORNER TRIANGLE
Row 1 (RS) K2, turn.
Row 2 (WS) P2, turn.
Row 3 Inc in first st by knitting into front and back of st, ssk, turn.
Row 4 P3, turn.
Row 5 Inc in first st, k1, ssk, turn.

Row 6 P4, turn.
Row 7 Inc in first st, k2, ssk, turn.
Row 8 P5, turn.
Row 9 Inc in first st, k3, ssk, turn.
Row 10 P6, turn.
Row 11 Inc in first st, k4, ssk, turn.
Row 12 P7, turn.
Row 13 Inc in first st, k5, ssk, turn.
Row 14 P8, turn.
Row 15 Inc in first st, k6, ssk, turn.
Row 16 P9, turn.
Row 17 Inc in first st, k7, ssk, do *not* turn.
The RH Corner Triangle is made. Leave 10 sts on RH needle.

RS RECTANGLES
*Pick-up row (RS) Pick up and k 10 sts evenly along edge of next triangle/rectangle, turn.
Row 1 (WS) P10 (this is row 2 of ridge pat on the right side), turn.
Row 2 P9, spp (with last st of rectangle and first st of next triangle/rectangle), turn.
Rows 3–20 Rep rows 1 and 2

nine times, keeping in ridge pat (on the right side) as established. Do *not* turn at end of last row.
NOTE On the knit (RS) rows, work skp and on the purl (RS) rows, work spp.
Rep from * across row—4 RS Rectangles have been made.

LH CORNER TRIANGLE
Pick-up row (RS) Pick up and k 10 sts along edge of last triangle/rectangle, turn.
Row 1 P2tog, p8, turn.
Row 2 K9, turn.
Row 3 P2tog, p7, turn.
Row 4 K8, turn.
Row 5 P2tog, p6, turn.
Row 6 K7, turn.
Row 7 P2tog, p5, turn.
Row 8 K6, turn.
Row 9 P2tog, p4, turn.
Row 10 K5, turn.
Row 11 P2tog, p3, turn.
Row 12 K4, turn.
Row 13 P2tog, p2, turn.
Row 14 K3, turn.
Row 15 P2tog, p1, turn.
Row 16 K2, turn.
Row 17 P2tog, do *not* turn—
1 st remains on RH needle.

WS RECTANGLES
Pick-up row (WS) Pick up and p 9 sts along edge of triangle just worked—10 sts, turn.

***Row 1 (RS)** P10 (row 2 of ridge pat on the wrong side), turn.
Row 2 P8, p2tog (with last st of rectangle and first st of next triangle/rectangle), turn.
Rows 3–20 Rep rows 1 and 2 nine times, keeping sts in ridge pat (on the wrong side) as established. Do *not* turn.
Next row (WS) Pick up and p 10 sts evenly along edge of next RS Rectangle.
Rep from * across row—5 WS Rectangles made. Turn.

Cont as established until 5 rows of RS Rectangles have been made, end with a LH Corner Triangle made.

END TRIANGLES
***Pick-up row (WS)** Pick up and p 9 sts evenly along edge of triangle just worked—10 sts on RH needle. Turn.
Row 1 (RS) K10, turn.
Row 2 P2tog, p7, p2tog, turn.
Row 3 K9, turn.
Row 4 P2tog, p6, p2tog, turn.
Row 5 K8, turn.
Row 6 P2tog, p5, p2tog, turn.
Row 7 K7, turn.
Row 8 P2tog, p4, p2tog, turn.
Row 9 K6, turn.
Row 10 P2tog, p3, p2tog, turn.
Row 11 K5, turn.
Row 12 P2tog, p2, p2tog, turn.

Row 13 K4, turn.
Row 14 P2tog, p1, p2tog, turn.
Row 15 K3, turn.
Row 16 P2tog, p2tog, turn.
Row 17 K2, turn.
Row 18 P2tog, p2tog, pass first st over 2nd st—1 st rem on RH needle.
Rep from * across row, picking up sts along edge of rectangle instead of triangle. Fasten off.

BACK
Cast on 50 sts and work in garter st for 6 rows for opening edge of bag.
Next row (WS) Purl.
Next row (RS) Beg ridge pat on WS and work until piece measures same as front. Bind off loosely.

I-CORD STRAP
With dpns, cast on 6 sts.
***Row 1 (RS)** K6. Do *not* turn.
Slide sts to beg of needle to work next row from RS. Rep from * until I-cord measures 32"/81cm. Bind off.

FINISHING
Block pieces to measurements. Sew side and bottom seams. Sew I-cord securely to inside of bag at each side seam. ❖

entre nous
Instead of working the back in ridge stitch, you could repeat the entrelac ridge pattern. You could also line the bag with a brightly colored fabric to use as a fun knitting bag.

INTERMEDIATE

sweet dreams baby blanket

Working a simple lace stitch into the entrelac pattern creates a design that looks more complex than it actually is. You'll wow everyone at the next baby shower.

FINISHED MEASUREMENTS
Approx 26" x 40"/66cm x 101.5cm

MATERIALS
■ 10 1¾oz/50g balls (each approx 137yd/125m) of Filatura Di Crosa/Tahki•Stacy Charles, Inc. *Zara* (extrafine merino) in #1392 pink (**3**)

■ One pair size 6 (4mm) needles OR SIZE TO OBTAIN GAUGE

GAUGE
12 sts = 2½"/6.5cm and 20 rows = 3"/7.5cm in lace chain pattern.
TAKE TIME TO CHECK GAUGE.

stitch

LACE CHAIN PATTERN
Panel of 10 sts

Row 1 and all WS rows Purl.
NOTE On row 7, work (k1, p1) into the double yarn over of previous row.
Row 2 K2, k2tog, yo, k2tog but do not slip from needle, insert RH needle between the sts just knitted together and k first st again; slip both sts from needle tog; yo, ssk, k2.
Row 4 K1, k2tog, yo, k4, yo, ssk, k1.
Row 6 K2tog, yo, k1, k2tog, (yo) twice, ssk, k1, yo, ssk.
Row 8 K2, yo, ssk, k2, k2tog, yo, k2.
Row 10 K3, yo, ssk, k2tog, yo, k3.
Rep rows 1–10 for lace chain pat.

NOTE An extra stitch is added to each side of the 10 sts in lace chain pat for the entrelac pattern.

BLANKET
Cast on 84 sts (multiple of 12 sts).

BASE TRIANGLES
*Row 1 (WS) P2, turn.
Row 2 (RS) K2, turn.
Row 3 P3, turn.
Row 4 K3, turn.
Row 5 P4, turn.
Row 6 K4, turn.
Row 7 P5, turn.
Row 8 K5, turn.
Row 9 P6, turn.
Row 10 K6, turn.
Row 11 P7, turn.
Row 12 K7, turn.
Row 13 P8, turn.
Row 14 K8, turn.
Row 15 P9, turn.
Row 16 K9, turn.
Row 17 P10, turn.
Row 18 K10, turn.
Row 19 P11, turn.
Row 20 K11, turn.
Row 21 P12, do *not* turn.
Rep from * for 6 more triangles—7 Base Triangles made. Turn.

RH CORNER TRIANGLE
Row 1 (RS) K2, turn.

Row 2 (WS) P2, turn.

Row 3 Inc in first st by knitting into front and back of st, ssk, turn.

Row 4 P3, turn.

Row 5 Inc in first st, k1, ssk, turn.

Row 6 P4, turn.

Row 7 Inc in first st, k2, ssk, turn.

Row 8 P5, turn.

Row 9 Inc in first st, k3, ssk, turn.

Row 10 P6, turn.

Row 11 Inc in first st, k4, ssk, turn.

Row 12 P7, turn.

Row 13 Inc in first st, k5, ssk, turn.

Row 14 P8, turn.

Row 15 Inc in first st, k6, ssk, turn.

Row 16 P9, turn.

Row 17 Inc in first st, k7, ssk, turn.

Row 18 P10, turn.

Row 19 Inc in first st, k8, ssk, turn.

Row 20 P11, turn.

Row 21 Inc in first st, k9, ssk, do *not* turn.

The RH Corner Triangle is made. Leave 12 sts on RH needle.

RS RECTANGLES

***Pick–up row (RS)** Pick up and k 12 sts evenly along edge of next triangle/rectangle, turn.

Row 1 (WS) Work row 1 of lace chain over 12 sts, turn.

Row 2 K1, work row 2 of lace chain over 10 sts, ssk (with last st of rectangle and first st of next triangle/rectangle), turn.

Row 3 Work row 3 of lace chain over 12 sts.

Row 4 K1, work row 4 of lace chain over 10 sts, ssk, turn.

Rows 5–24 Rep rows 3 and 4, keeping center 10 sts in lace chain pat as established. Do *not* turn at end of last row.

Rep from * across row—6 RS Rectangles have been made.

LH CORNER TRIANGLE

Pick–up row (RS) Pick up and k 12 sts along edge of last triangle/rectangle, turn.

Row 1 P2tog, p10, turn.

Row 2 K11, turn.

Row 3 P2tog, p9, turn.

Row 4 K10, turn.

Row 5 P2tog, p8, turn.

Row 6 K9, turn.

Row 7 P2tog, p7, turn.

Row 8 K8, turn.

Row 9 P2tog, p6, turn.

Row 10 K7, turn.

Row 11 P2tog, p5, turn.

Row 12 K6, turn.

Row 13 P2tog, p4, turn.

Row 14 K5, turn.

Row 15 P2tog, p3, turn.

Row 16 K4, turn.

Row 17 P2tog, p2, turn.

Row 18 K3, turn.

Row 19 P2tog, p1, turn.

Row 20 K2, turn.

Row 21 P2tog, do *not* turn—1 st remains on RH needle.

entre nous

For a baby boy, use a different color of yarn and substitute the lace pattern with a textured pattern, such as a simple cable. See pages 40 to 43 for lots of options.

WS RECTANGLES

Pick–up row (WS) Pick up and p 11 sts evenly along edge of triangle just worked—12 sts, turn.

***Row 1** K1, work row 2 of lace chain over 10 sts, k1, turn.

Row 2 P11, p2tog (with last st of rectangle and first st of next triangle/rectangle), turn.

Rows 3–22 Rep rows 1 and 2, keeping center 10 sts in lace chain pat as established.

Row 23 K12, turn.

Row 24 Rep row 2, do *not* turn.

Next row (WS) Pick up and p 12 sts evenly along edge of next RS Rectangle.

Rep from * across row—7 WS Rectangles have been made. Turn.

Cont as established until 12 rows of RS Rectangles have been worked, ending with a LH Corner Triangle.

END TRIANGLES

***Pick–up row (WS)** Pick up and p 11 sts evenly along edge of triangle just worked—12 sts on RH needle. Turn.

Row 1 (RS) K12, turn.

Row 2 P2tog, p9, p2tog, turn.

Row 3 K11, turn.

Row 4 P2tog, p8, p2tog, turn.

Row 5 K10, turn.

Row 6 P2tog, p7, p2tog, turn.

Row 7 K9, turn.

Row 8 P2tog, p6, p2tog, turn.

Row 9 K8, turn.

Row 10 P2tog, p5, p2tog, turn.

Row 11 K7, turn.

Row 12 P2tog, p4, p2tog, turn.

Row 13 K6, turn.

Row 14 P2tog, p3, p2tog, turn.

Row 15 K5, turn.

Row 16 P2tog, p2, p2tog, turn.

Row 17 K4, turn.

Row 18 P2tog, p1, p2tog, turn.

Row 19 K3, turn.

Row 20 P2tog, p2tog, turn.

Row 21 K2, turn.

Row 22 P2tog, p2tog, pass first st over 2nd st—1 st remains on RH needle.

Rep from * across row, picking up sts along edge of rectangle instead of triangle.

Fasten off rem st.

FINISHING

Block to measurements. ❖

EXPERIENCED

geometric motifs blanket

The designs on Barbara Venishnick's blanket were inspired by the mudcloth textiles and painted mud-and-wattle houses of the Ndebele in southern Africa.

FINISHED MEASUREMENTS
56" x 72"/142cm x 183cm

MATERIALS
- 13 1¾oz/50g hanks (each approx 120yd/108m) of Classic Elite Yarns *Portland Tweed* (wool/alpaca/viscose) in #5078 espresso (MC) (4)
- 8 hanks in #5036 desert sand (A)
- 3 hanks each in #5058 ruby red (B) and #5085 yam (C)
- 2 hanks in #5097 green tea (D)
- Size 7 (4.5mm) jumper needle (or 2 circular needles with rubber stoppers added to one end of each needle)
- Size G/6 (4.5mm) crochet hook

GAUGE
17½ sts and 30½ rows = 4"/10cm over purl or knit garter st using size 7 (4.5mm) needles. TAKE TIME TO CHECK GAUGE.

note
Striped squares are worked in purl garter (p every row) and charted squares are worked in knit garter (k every row).

AFGHAN
STRIPED (BASE) RECTANGLES (1)
With A, cast on 32 sts. P 1 row. [P 2 rows MC. P 2 rows A] 15 times. P 2 rows MC—63 rows. Cut yarn and leave rectangle on needle. Make 4 more rectangles in the same way, casting sts onto free needle, but on the last (5th) rectangle bind off 32 sts and cut yarn.

RS RECTANGLES
Beg Rectangle 2 Chart
With the RS facing of the last (5th) rectangle, free needle and MC, pick up and k 32 sts along the left side of the rectangle. Sl the first st of the next striped rectangle from the LH needle to the RH needle and pass the last picked-up st over it, turn.
*Next row (WS) Work row 2 (first row, and read from left to right) of chart, turn.
Next row (RS) Work row 3 (2nd row, and read from right to left) of chart through st 31, k tog the last st of rectangle with the next st of Striped Rectangle, turn. Rep from *, keeping in chart pat, through row 63. Do *not* turn at end of row 63. Cut yarn. Leave this rectangle on RH needle.

Beg Rectangle 3 Chart
Next row (RS) Pick up and k 32 sts of Striped Rectangle just joined as foll: 7 sts C, 5 sts MC, 20 sts B. Work as for Rectangle 2, only foll Rectangle 3 chart. Cont in this way, working Rectangle 4, then Rectangle 5, following corresponding charts (see placement diagram) and on pick-up row, use colors foll row 1 of chart. Leave all rectangles on LH needle. Turn.

WS RECTANGLES
(worked in striped pat as on Rectangle 1)
Next row (WS) With WS facing and completed rectangles on LH needle and A, cast 32 sts onto free needle. Sl first st of Rectangle 5 to RH needle and pass last cast-on st over it, turn.
*Next row (RS) P 1 row A, turn.
Next row (WS) Purl with MC to last st and p it tog with next st of Rectangle 5, turn. Rep from *, keeping in stripe pat, until 32 sts of Rectangle 5 have been worked. Work 1 more row on WS, turn. With WS facing, slide 32 sts of rectangle just worked to RH needle. With RH needle and A, pick up and p 32 sts along other side of rectangle 5 and work another Striped Rectangle. Sl first st of Rectangle to RH needle and pass last picked-up st over it, turn. Rep from * of WS Rectangle (see diagram for

96

placement), until there are 5 rectangles made. Bind off 32 sts of last (5th) rectangle. Cont to alternate RS rows of charted rectangles and WS row of striped rectangles, foll placement diagram, and bind off the 32 sts of each final (corner) rectangle.

FINISHING

With RS facing, MC and crochet hook, work 1 sc in every cast-on or bound-off st and 1 sc in every other row (each garter ridge), working a ch-3 lp at each corner of the striped rectangles.

TASSELS

With 1 strand of MC and A held tog, make 22 tassels as foll: Wrap yarn around a 6"/15.5cm piece of cardboard 14 times. Cut one end and pull through the ch-3 lp, fold in half and wrap tightly with color B, C or D to form tassel. ❖

This modified-entrelac afghan uses Base, End and Corner Rectangles instead of Triangles.

Placement Key

1 Striped Rectangle

2 Rectangle 2

3 Rectangle 3

4 Rectangle 4

5 Rectangle 5

PLACEMENT DIAGRAM

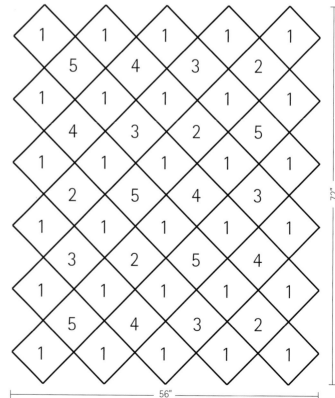

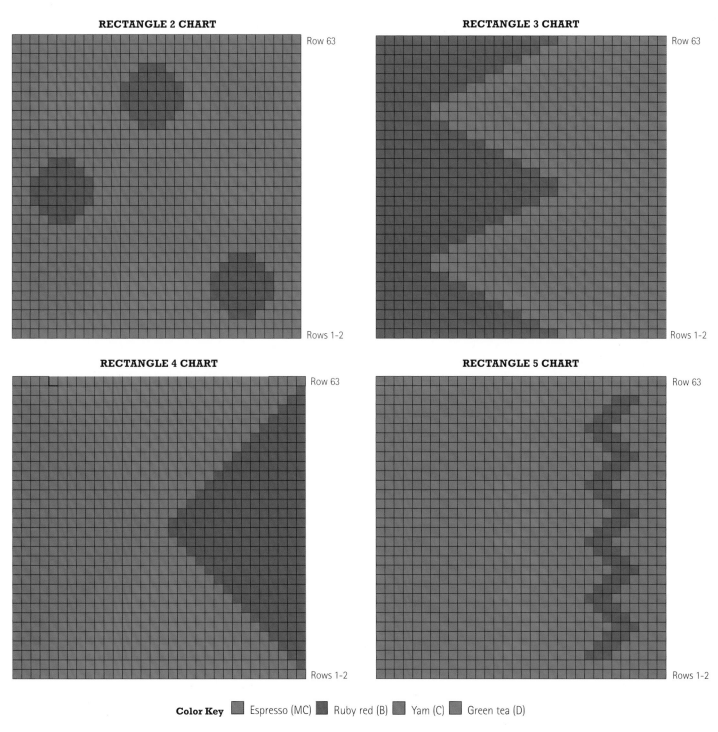

RECTANGLE 2 CHART

Row 63

Rows 1-2

RECTANGLE 3 CHART

Row 63

Rows 1-2

RECTANGLE 4 CHART

Row 63

Rows 1-2

RECTANGLE 5 CHART

Row 63

Rows 1-2

Color Key ■ Espresso (MC) ■ Ruby red (B) ■ Yam (C) ■ Green tea (D)

NOTE: Each row of chart represents 2 rows of knitting, except row 63. All charts are worked in knit garter (k every row).

EXPERIENCED

rose garden baby cardi

What could be sweeter than a pint-sized cardigan bordered with entrelac and tiny embroidered rosebuds?

SIZES

Sized for 6–9 months (9–12 months, 12–18 months); shown in size 6–9 months.

FINISHED MEASUREMENTS

Chest (buttoned) 23 (24½, 25)"/58 (62, 65.5)cm
Length 11 (11½, 12)"/28 (29, 30.5)cm

MATERIALS

■ 3 (3, 4) 1¾oz/50g balls (each approx 181yd/166m) of Filatura Di Crosa/Tahki•Stacy Charles, Inc. *Zarina* (wool) in #1510 pink **2**
■ One pair size 3 (3.25mm) needles OR SIZE TO OBTAIN GAUGE
■ 1 (2, 2) skein of DMC *#5 Perle Cotton* in #893 dark pink
■ 1 skein each in #818 light pink and #503 green
■ Crochet hook size B/1 (2.25mm)
■ Three ¾"/20mm buttons
■ Stitch markers and holders

GAUGE

26 sts and 33 rows = 4"/10cm over St st using size 3 (3.25mm) needles.
TAKE TIME TO CHECK GAUGE.

LEFT FRONT

Cast on 40 (42, 44) sts. Work in St st for 3½ (4, 4)"/9 (10, 10)cm, end with a WS row.

SLEEVE

Next row (RS) Cast on 28 (30, 32) sts for sleeve, k to end—68 (72, 76) sts. Cont in St st until piece measures 6½ (7, 7½)"/16.5 (17.5, 19)cm from beg, end with a RS row.

SHAPE NECK

Next row (WS) Bind off 6 sts (neck edge), work to end. Cont to bind off from neck edge 2 sts twice, dec 1 st every other row 3 times—55 (59, 63) sts. Work even, if necessary, until piece measures 8 (8½, 9)"/20.5 (21.5, 23)cm from beg. Place sts on a holder.

RIGHT FRONT

Work to correspond to Left Front, reversing all shaping.

SLEEVES AND BACK

Next row (RS) Work 55 (59, 63) sts from Left Front and Sleeve holder, cast on 26 sts for back neck, work 55 (59, 63) sts from Right Front and Sleeve holder—136 (144, 152) sts. Place markers each end of row for shoulders. Work even until sleeves measure 4½ (4½, 5)"/11.5 (11.5, 12.5)cm above shoulder markers. Bind off 28 (30, 32) sts at beg of next 2 rows—80 (84, 88) sts. Work even until back measures same length as fronts. Bind off all sts.

ENTRELAC BAND FOR LOWER EDGE (MAKE 2)

Cast on 15 sts (multiple of 5 sts).

BASE TRIANGLES

*Row 1 (WS) P2, turn.
Row 2 (RS) K2, turn.
Row 3 P3, turn.
Row 4 K3, turn.
Row 5 P4, turn.
Row 6 K4, turn.
Row 7 P5, do *not* turn.
Rep from * twice more—3 Base Triangles have been worked. Turn.

RH CORNER TRIANGLE

Row 1 (RS) K2, turn.
Row 2 (WS) P2, turn.
Row 3 Inc in first st by knitting into front and back of st, ssk, turn.
Row 4 P3 turn.
Row 5 Inc in first st, k1, ssk, turn.
Row 6 P4, turn.
Row 7 Inc in first st, k2, ssk, do *not* turn. The RH Corner Triangle is complete. Leave 5 sts on RH needle.

RS RECTANGLES

*Pick-up row (RS) Pick up and k 5 sts evenly along edge of next triangle/rectangle, turn.
Row 1 (WS) P5, turn.
Row 2 K4, ssk (with last st of rectangle and first st of next triangle/rectangle), turn.
Rows 3–10 Rep rows 1 and 2 four times. Do *not* turn at end of last row.

Rep from * across row—2 RS Rectangles have been made.

LH CORNER TRIANGLE

Pick-up row (RS) Pick up and k 5 sts along edge of last triangle/rectangle, turn.
Row 1 P2tog, p3, turn.
Row 2 K4, turn.
Row 3 P2tog, p2, turn.
Row 4 K3, turn.
Row 5 P2tog, p1, turn.
Row 6 K2, turn.
Row 7 P2tog, do *not* turn—1 st remains on RH needle.

WS RECTANGLES

Pick-up row (WS) Pick up and p 4 sts evenly along edge of triangle just worked—5 sts on RH needle, turn.
*Row 1 K5, turn.
Row 2 P4, p2tog (with last st of rectangle and first st of next triangle/rectangle), turn.
Rows 3–10 Rep rows 1 and 2 four times. Do *not* turn.
Next row (WS) Pick up and p 5 sts evenly along edge of next RS rectangle. Rep from * across row—3 WS Rectangles have been made. Turn.
****Work 1 RH Corner Triangle. Work 1 row of RS Rectangles. Do *not* turn.
Work 1 LH Corner Triangle.
Work 1 row of WS Rectangles.
Rep from ** until piece measures approx 10½ (11¾, 12¾)"/26.5 (30, 35)cm from beg, end with a LH Corner Triangle.

END TRIANGLES

*Pick-up row (WS) Pick up and p 4 sts evenly along edge of triangle just worked—5 sts. Turn.
Row 1 (RS) K5, turn.
Row 2 P2tog, p2, p2tog, turn.
Row 3 K4, turn.
Row 4 P2tog, p1, p2tog, turn.
Row 5 K3, turn.
Row 6 P2tog, p2tog, turn.
Row 7 K2, turn.
Row 8 P2tog, p2tog, pass 1st st over 2nd st—1 st remains on needle. Do *not* turn.
Rep from * across row, picking up sts along edge of rectangle instead of triangle.
Fasten off rem st.

ENTRELAC SLEEVE BANDS (MAKE 2)

Cast on 45 (45, 50) sts and work 9 (9, 10) Base Triangles (5 sts each as before).
Work 1 RH Corner Triangle, 8 (8, 9) RS Rectangles, 1 LH Corner Triangle and 9 (9, 10) End Triangles.

EMBROIDERY

On Sleeve Bands, work 1 rose with bullion sts and 2 lazy daisy st leaves (see illustrations below and photo on opposite page) in each RS Rectangle. On Front Bands, work 1 rose in each WS Rectangle on RS of work. Work 2 roses on each side of neck (see photo).

FINISHING

Block pieces to measurements. Sew entrelac bands to sleeves. Sew side and sleeve seams. Sew one long side of entrelac band to lower Right Front and one half of Back edge, easing to fit. Sew 2nd entrelac band to Left Front and one half Back edge in same way. Sew back seam of bands.

EDGING

With RS facing and crochet hook, beg at lower edge of Right Front, work a row of sc along Right Front, Back Neck and Left Front edge, working 3 sc in same st at corner of each neck edge on fronts. Turn, and sc in each sc, working button loops (ch 2, skip 2 sc for each loop) along Right Front, working 1 loop at 3 sc down from neck edge and the other two at 5 sc apart. Sew on buttons opposite button loops. ❖

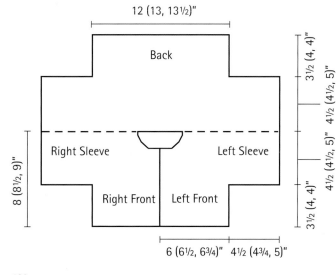

12 (13, 13½)"

Back

3½ (4, 4)"

4½ (4½, 5)"

Right Sleeve   Left Sleeve

8 (8½, 9)"

Right Front   Left Front

3½ (4, 4)"

6 (6½, 6¾)"   4½ (4¾, 5)"

BULLION STITCH

LAZY DAISY STITCH

EXPERIENCED

edwardian cardigan

Kathy Merrick combined an amazing nine shades of yarn in this stunning garment. The rich tones of the yarn and the peplum silhouette give it a demure look.

SIZES

Sized for Woman's Medium (Large). Shown in size Large.

FINISHED MEASUREMENTS

Bust 40½ (50½)"/103 (128)cm

Length 19½"/49.5cm

Upper arm 13"/33cm

MATERIALS

■ 2 1¾oz/50g skeins (each approx 176yd/160m) each of Koigu Wool Designs *Koigu Premium Merino* (wool) in #P4000 black/green (A), #P3005 bright purple (B), #P1045 light blue (C), #P2239 burgundy (D), #P1110 rust (E), #P1305 taupe (F), #P3000 royal purple (G), #P1040 teal (H) and #P2340 light olive (I) **1**

■ One pair size 4 (3.5mm) needles OR SIZE TO OBTAIN GAUGE

■ Size 6 (4mm) circular needle, 32"/81cm long OR SIZE TO OBTAIN GAUGE

■ Five ⅝"/16mm buttons

GAUGES

■ 26 sts and 34 rows = 4"/10cm over St st, using size 4 (3.5mm) needles.

■ 24 sts and 36 rows = 4"/10cm over St st, using size 6 (4mm) needles.
TAKE TIME TO CHECK GAUGES.

STRIPE SEQUENCES (BODY)

STRIPE SEQUENCE 1
*1 row A, 1 row B, 1 row C; rep from *.

STRIPE SEQUENCE 2
*1 row D, 1 row E, 1 row F; rep from *.

STRIPE SEQUENCE 3
*1 row G, 1 row H, 1 row I; rep from *.

LOWER BODY

BASE TRIANGLES

With circular needle and A, cast on 198 (234) sts (a multiple of 9 sts). Work in stripe sequence 1 as foll:
*Row 1 (RS) With A, k2, turn.
Row 2 (WS) With B, p2, turn.
Row 3 With C, k3, turn.
Row 4 With A, p3, turn.
Row 5 With B, k4, turn.
Row 6 With C, p4, turn.
Row 7 With A, k5, turn.
Row 8 With B, p5, turn.
Row 9 With C, k6, turn.
Row 10 With A, p6, turn.
Row 11 With B, k7, turn.
Row 12 With C, p7, turn.
Row 13 With A, k8, turn.
Row 14 With B, p8, turn.
Row 15 With C (stranding B across), k9, do *not* turn.
Rep from * for 21 (25) more triangles—22 (26) Base Triangles made. Cut yarn.
Turn.

Work next row of triangles/rectangles in stripe sequence 2 as foll:

LH CORNER TRIANGLE
Row 1 (WS) With D, p2, turn.
Row 2 (RS) With E, k1, M1, k1, turn.
Row 3 With F, p2, p2tog (with last st of triangle and first st of next triangle/rectangle), turn.
Row 4 With D, k2, M1, k1, turn.
Row 5 With E, p3, p2tog, turn.
Row 6 With F, k3, M1, k1, turn.
Row 7 With D, p4, p2tog, turn.
Row 8 With E, k4, M1, k1, turn.
Row 9 With F, p5, p2tog, turn.
Row 10 With D, k5, M1, k1, turn.
Row 11 With E, p6, p2tog, turn.
Row 12 With F, k6, M1, k1, turn.
Row 13 With D, p7, p2tog, turn.
Row 14 With E, k7, M1, k1, turn.

notes

1 Cardigan body is worked in one piece to armholes, then divided for fronts and back.

2 Each complete row of triangles/rectangles uses a different stripe sequence.

3 Do not cut yarn after each row of a stripe sequence; carry colors along sides until needed again. Cut yarn after a stripe sequence has been completed.

4 When finishing a triangle/rectangle, strand 2nd color of stripe sequence across last row so it is in place for the next block.

5 Work pick-up row for triangle/rectangle with 3rd color of stripe sequence. Strand first color of stripe sequence across pick up row so it is in place for next row.

6 Use knit-on cast-on throughout.

LOWER BODY

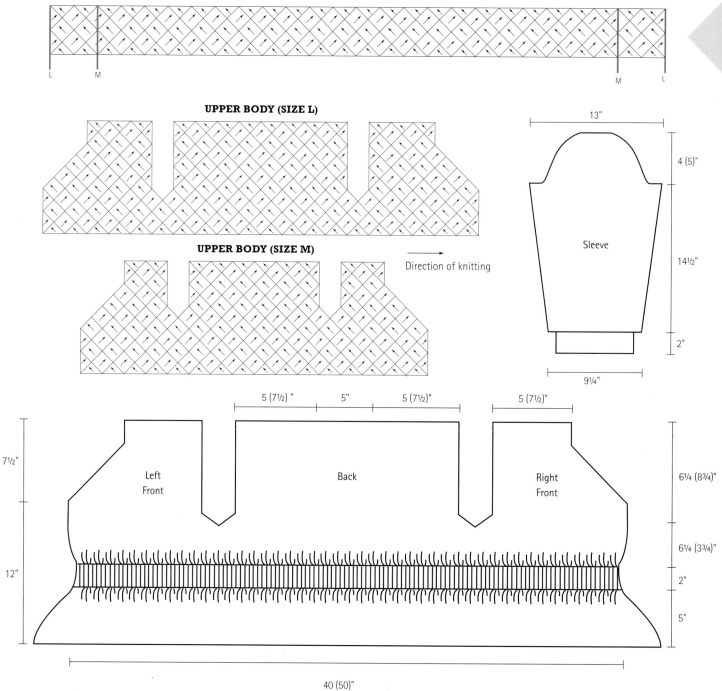

UPPER BODY (SIZE L)

UPPER BODY (SIZE M)

Direction of knitting

13"

4 (5)"

Sleeve

14½"

2"

9¼"

5 (7½) "   5"   5 (7½)"   5 (7½)"

7½"

Left
Front

Back

Right
Front

6¼ (8¾)"

6¼ (3¾)"

2"

12"

5"

40 (50)"

Row 15 With F (stranding E across), p8, p2tog, do *not* turn.

WS RECTANGLES

*Pick-up row (WS) With F (stranding D across), pick up and p 9 sts evenly along edge of triangle/rectangle, turn.
Row 1 (RS) With D, k9, turn.
Row 2 With E, p8, p2tog, turn.
Rows 3–18 Rep last 2 rows 8 times (cont working stripe sequence as established). Do *not* turn. Strand E across on last row. Rep from * for 20 (24) more rectangles—21 (25) WS Rectangles made.

RH CORNER TRIANGLE

Pick-up row (WS) With F (stranding D), pick up and p9 sts evenly along edge of last triangle/rectangle, turn.
Row 1 (RS) With D, k9, turn.
Row 2 With E, p7, p2tog, turn.
Row 3 With F, k8, turn.
Row 4 With D, p6, p2tog, turn.
Row 5 With E, k7, turn.
Row 6 With F, p5, p2tog, turn.
Row 7 With D, k6, turn.
Row 8 With E, p4, p2tog, turn.
Row 9 With F, k5, turn.
Row 10 With D, p3, p2tog, turn.
Row 11 With E, k4, turn.
Row 12 With F, p2, p2tog, turn.
Row 13 With D, k3, turn.
Row 14 With E, p1, p2tog, turn.

Row 15 With F, k2, turn.
Row 16 With D, p2tog, sl rem st to RH needle. Turn. Cut yarn.

Work in stripe sequence 3 as foll:
RS RECTANGLES
Pick-up row (RS) With I, pick up and k 8 sts evenly along edge of triangle—9 sts on RH needle, turn.
***Row 1 (WS)** With G, p 9.
Row 2 With H, k8, ssk, turn.
Rows 3–18 Rep last 2 rows 8 times (cont working stripe sequence as established). Do *not* turn. Strand H across on last row.
Pick-up row (RS) With I (stranding G across), pick up and k 9 sts evenly along edge of next rectangle.
Rep from * for 21 (25) more rectangles (omitting last pick-up row on last rectangle)—22 (26) RS Rectangles made. Cut yarn. Turn.

Work in stripe sequence 1 as foll:
Work 1 LH Triangle.
Work 21 (25) WS Rectangles.
Work 1 RH Triangle.

END TRIANGLES
Work in stripe sequence 2 as foll (stranding colors as needed):
***Pick-up row (RS)** With F, pick up and k 8 sts evenly along edge of triangle/rectangle—9 sts on RH needle, turn.
Row 1 (WS) With D, p9, turn.

Row 2 With E, k8, ssk, turn.
Row 3 With F, p8, wrap next st, turn.
Row 4 With D, k7, ssk, turn.
Row 5 With E, p7, wrap next st, turn.
Row 6 With F, k6, ssk, turn.
Row 7 With D, p6, wrap next st, turn.
Row 8 With E, k5, ssk, turn.
Row 9 With F, p5, wrap next st, turn.
Row 10 With D, k4, ssk, turn.
Row 11 With E, p4, wrap next st, turn.
Row 12 With F, k3, ssk, turn.
Row 13 With D, p3, wrap next st, turn.
Row 14 With E, k2, ssk, turn.
Row 15 With F, p2, wrap next st, turn.
Row 16 With D, k1, ssk, turn.
Row 17 With E, p1, wrap next st, turn.
Row 18 With F, ssk, do *not* turn—1 st remains.
Rep from * for 21 (25) more triangles—22 (26) End Triangles made. Turn.
Next row (WS) With D, purl across 198 (234) sts, hiding all wraps. Cut yarn.

WAIST RIBBING
Dec row (RS) With G, k6 (5) [k2tog, k3 (4)] 38 times, k2 (1)—160 (196) sts.

Work in k1, p1 rib in the foll color sequence:
1 row G, 2 rows each with H, I, A, B, C, D and E, then 1 row F.
Dec row (WS): Size M With F, p11, [p2tog, p7] 16 times, p5—144 sts.
Size L With F, p10, [p2tog, p10] 5 times, [p2tog, p9] 6 times, [p2tog, p10] 5 times—180 sts.

UPPER BODY (SIZE M)
NOTE Foll diagrams for upper body.
Work 16 base triangles, using stripe sequence 3.
Cont to alternate stripe sequences as established, work as foll:
**Work 1 LH Triangle, 15 WS Rectangles, and 1 RH Triangle.
Work 16 RS Rectangles.
Rep from ** once more.
Bind off 9 sts of first RS Rectangle. Work 15 WS Rectangles.

DIVIDE FOR BACK AND FRONTS
RIGHT FRONT
Bind off 9 sts of first WS Rectangle. Work 3 RS Rectangles. Work 1 LH Triangle and 2 WS Rectangles.
Bind off 9 sts of first WS Rectangle. Work 2 RS Rectangles. Work 1 LH Triangle, 1 WS Rectangle, and 1 RH Triangle.

END TRIANGLES

*Pick-up row (RS) Pick up and k 8 sts evenly along edge of triangle/rectangle—9 sts on RH needle, turn.

Row 1 (WS) P9, turn.
Row 2 Ssk, k6, ssk, turn.
Row 3 P8, turn.
Row 4 Ssk, k5, ssk, turn.
Row 5 P7, turn.
Row 6 Ssk, k4, ssk, turn.
Row 7 P6, turn.
Row 8 Ssk, k3, ssk, turn.
Row 9 P5, turn.
Row 10 Ssk, k2, ssk, turn.
Row 11 P4, turn.
Row 12 Ssk, k1, ssk, turn.
Row 13 P3, turn.
Row 14 [Ssk] twice, turn.
Row 15 P2, turn.
Row 16 K1, ssk, turn.
Row 17 P2, turn.
Row 18 SK2P, do *not* turn—1 st remains.
Rep from * for 1 more triangle—2 End Triangles made. Fasten off last st.

BACK

Bind off 9 sts of first WS Rectangle.
**Work 6 RS Rectangles.
Work 1 LH Triangle, 5 WS Rectangles, and 1 RH Triangle.
Rep from ** once more.
Work 6 End Triangles.

LEFT FRONT

Bind off 9 sts of first WS Rectangle. Work 3 RS Rectangles.
Bind off 9 sts of first RS Rectangle. Work 2 WS Rectangles and 1 RH Triangle.
Work 2 RS Rectangles.
Work 1 LH Triangle, 1 WS Rectangle and 1 RH Triangle.
Work 2 End Triangles. Fasten off.

UPPER BODY (SIZE L)

Work 20 Base Triangles, using stripe sequence 3.

Cont to alternate stripe sequences as established, work as foll:
Work 1 LH triangle, 19 WS rectangles and 1 RH triangle.
Work 20 RS Rectangles.
Work 1 LH Triangle, 19 WS Rectangles, and 1 RH Triangle.

DIVIDE FOR BACK AND FRONTS
RIGHT FRONT

Work 5 RS Rectangles.
Work 1 LH Triangle and 4 WS Rectangles.
Bind off 9 sts of first WS Rectangle. Work 4 RS Rectangles.
Work 1 LH Triangle and 3 WS Rectangles.
Bind off 9 sts of first WS Rectangle. Work 3 RS Rectangles.
Work 1 LH Triangle, 2 WS Rectangles, and 1 RH Triangle.
Work 3 End Triangles as for size M.

BACK

Bind off 9 sts of first WS Rectangle.
**Work 8 RS Rectangles.
Work 1 LH Triangle, 7 WS Rectangles, and 1 RH Triangle.
Rep from ** twice more.
Work 8 End Triangles.

LEFT FRONT

Bind off 9 sts of first WS Rectangle. Work 5 RS Rectangles.
Bind off 9 sts of first RS Rectangle. Work 4 WS Rectangles and 1 RH Triangle.
Work 4 RS Rectangles.
Bind off 9 sts of first RS Rectangle. Work 3 WS Rectangles and 1 RH Triangle.
Work 3 RS Rectangles.
Work 1 LH Triangle, 2 WS Rectangles, and 1 RH Triangle.
Work 3 End Triangles. Fasten off.

SLEEVES

With straight needles and A, cast on 60 sts. Work in k1, p1 rib in the foll stripe sequence: 2 rows each A, B, C, D, E, F, G, H and I. Change to St st and rep 18-row stripe sequence, AT SAME TIME, inc 1 st each side every 10th row 12 times—84 sts. Work even until piece measures 16½"/42cm from beg, end with a WS row.

SHAPE CAP

Bind off 7 sts at beg of next 2 rows. Dec 1 st each side every RS row 11 (20) times. Work 1 row even. Bind off 2 sts at beg of next 4 (2) rows, 3 sts at beg of next 8 (2) rows. Bind off rem 16 (20) sts.

FINISHING

Sew shoulder seams. Set in sleeves. Sew sleeve seams.

EDGING

With RS facing, circular needle and A, beg at lower Right Front and pick up and k 52 sts to beg of neck shaping, 48 sts to shoulder, 36 sts along back neck, 48 sts to beg of Left Front neck shaping, and 52 sts to lower Left Front edge—236 sts. K 2 rows.
Buttonhole row (WS) K to last 52 sts, yo, k2tog, [k8, yo, k2tog] 4 times, k10.
K 2 rows. Bind off.
Sew on buttons opposite buttonholes. ❖

EASY

tweed beret

Kay Niederlitz knit this cozy beret in five shades of tweed yarn to create a patchwork look. The hat fits loosely for a slouchy effect that allows you to wear it at different angles. *C'est magnifique!*

SIZE
Sized for adult woman.

MATERIALS
■ 1 3½oz/100g skein (approx183yd/167m) each of Tahki Yarns/Tahki•Stacy Charles, Inc. *Donegal Tweed* (wool) in #848 cream (A), #830 fawn (B), #894 dark green (C), #839 dark khaki (D) and #890 black (E) **(4)**

■ Two sets (10) size 8 (5mm) double-pointed needles (dpns) OR SIZE TO OBTAIN GAUGE

■ One size 6 (4mm) circular needle, 16"/40cm long OR SIZE TO OBTAIN GAUGE

■ Stitch markers

■ Stitch holders

■ Tapestry needle

GAUGE
16 sts and 24 rows = 4"/10cm over St st using size 8 (5mm) needles.
TAKE TIME TO CHECK GAUGE.

BERET
CENTER TOP (CROWN)
With A and dpns, cast on 9 sts. Divide evenly on 3 needles. Join, taking care not to twist sts on needles.

Rnd 1 Inc into first and last st on each needle by knitting into front and back (k1fb) of st— 15 sts.

Rnd 2 Knit 15 sts.

Rnd 3 Inc 9 sts evenly in round by knitting into front and back of 1st, 3rd and 5th st on each needle—24 sts.

Rnd 4 Knit 24 sts.

Rnd 5 K1fb of 1st st , k2, k1fb of next st, k1, k1fb of next st, k1, k1fb of next st—12 sts on needle; inc in same manner on next 2 needles—36 sts.

Rnd 6 K 36 sts.

Rnd 7 K1fb of 1st st, k3, k1fb of next st, k3, k1fb of next st, k2, k1fb of last st on needle— 16 sts. Work next 2 needles in same manner—48 sts. Divide sts onto 4 dpns (12 sts on each needle).

Rnd 8 K 48 sts.

Rnd 9 Inc 12 sts evenly spaced around—60 sts.

Rnds 10–12 K 60.

Rnd 13 Inc 10 sts evenly spaced around—70 sts.

Rnds 14–16 Knit.

Rnd 17 Inc 10 sts evenly spaced around—80 sts.

Rnds 18–20 Knit.

NOTE You will now begin to work back and forth using 8 dpns, working with the 9th needle.

FOUNDATION TRIANGLE 1 (COLOR B; OVER 10 STS)
Row 1 (RS) With a free dpn and color B, k2, turn work, p2, turn work, k3, turn, p3, turn, cont in this way, adding one more st every RS row, until 10 sts have been worked onto RH needle. Leave sts on hold.

FOUNDATION TRIANGLE 2 (OVER 10 STS)
Work as for triangle 1 over the next 10 sts.
Work 6 more triangles in same

notes
1 Center top of hat is worked in the round until entrelac pat begins, when it is worked in rows on dpns.
2 Use stitch markers to mark ends of rnds.
3 On row after picking up stitches, knit or purl through back loop to avoid having a gap between picked-up stitches and rectangle.

manner, so that all 80 sts have been worked onto 8 dpns (10 sts per needle).

FIRST ROW OF RECTANGLES (COLOR C)

RECTANGLE 1

NOTE This row of rectangles is worked clockwise.

With WS facing and C, beg with Triangle 1, pick up and p 10 sts along right edge of Triangle 1. Sl last st picked up to LH needle. P2tog, turn.

*Next row (RS) K10, turn.

Next row P9, p2tog, turn. Rep from * until all 10 sts from triangle have been worked. One rectangle is formed and joined to the left side of Triangle 8.

RECTANGLE 2

With WS facing and C, pick up and p 10 sts along right edge of triangle 8. Sl last st picked up to LH needle. P2tog, turn. Rep from * of Rectangle 1.

Cont in this manner, working 6 more rectangles along the Base Triangles.

entre nous

Feeling sunny? For a change of season (or mood!), substitute bright oranges and yellows for more subdued colors as shown above.

SECOND ROW OF RECTANGLES (COLOR D)

RECTANGLE 1

NOTE This row of rectangles is worked counterclockwise.

With RS facing and D, pick up and k 10 sts along side of first rectangle from first row of rectangles.

*Row 1 (WS) P10, turn.

Row 2 (RS) K9, SKP, turn.

Rep from * until all 10 sts from rectangle have been worked. Work 7 more rectangles in this manner.

LAST ROW OF TRIANGLES (COLOR E)

NOTE This row of triangles is worked clockwise.

TRIANGLE 1

With WS facing and color E, pick up and p 10 sts along side edge of first rectangle from second row of rectangles. Sl last st picked up to LH needle. P2tog, turn.

Next row (RS) K9, wyib, sl the 10th st to RH needle, bring yarn to front, sl st back to LH needle, turn.

Next row P8, p2tog, turn.

Next row (RS) K8, wyib, sl the 9th st to RH needle, bring yarn to front, sl st back to LH needle, turn.

Next row P7, p2tog, turn.

Cont in this manner, working 1 less st every other row until all 10 sts from rectangle have been worked.

Work 7 more triangles in this manner. There are now 10 sts on each needle, or 80 sts in total.

BRIM

With circular needle, k 1 rnd, picking up wraps at each turn, and k the wrap tog with st on LH needle to close up holes. Join and cont to work in rounds of k1, p1 rib for 8 rnds. Bind off in rib.

FINISHING

With tapestry needle, draw cast-on end of yarn through cast-on sts and pull together to close hole. Weave in ends. ❖

EASY

quick-knit kerchief

A simple triangular piece becomes a boho-chic accessory that you can wear around your head or around your neck, bandanna-style.

SIZE
Sized for adult woman.

FINISHED MEASUREMENTS
10" x 22"/25.5cm x 56cm

MATERIALS
- 2 1¾oz/50g skeins (each approx 146yd/135m) of Tahki Yarns/Tahki•Stacy Charles, Inc. *Cotton Classic Lite* (cotton) in #4870 blue (3)
- One pair size 4 (3.5mm) needles OR SIZE TO OBTAIN GAUGE
- One ¾"/20mm button

GAUGE
24 sts and 32 rows = 4"/10cm over St st using size 4 (3.5mm) needles.
TAKE TIME TO CHECK GAUGE.

KERCHIEF
Cast on 6 sts. Work in St st for 12 rows.

RS RECTANGLES
Next row (RS) Cast on 6 sts. [K5, ssk, turn. P6, turn] 5 times. K5, ssk. Do *not* turn.
Pick-up row (RS) Pick up and k 6 sts evenly along edge of first rectangle.
Work 12 rows in St st on these 6 sts. Turn.

WS RECTANGLES
Next row (WS) Cast on 6 sts. Do *not* turn.
[P5, p2tog, turn. K6, turn] 5 times. P5, p2tog. Do *not* turn.
Pick-up row (WS) Pick up and p 6 sts evenly along edge of next rectangle, turn.
K6, turn.
[P5, p2tog, turn. K6, turn] 5 times. P5, p2tog. Do *not* turn.
Pick up and p 6 sts along edge of next rectangle. Turn.

entre nous
Turn this little kerchief into a luxurious shawl by using a fine mohair yarn and continuing the pattern until the triangle is the size you want. You could also cast on more stitches to create larger rectangles.

Work in St st for 12 rows. Turn.
Next row (RS) Cast on 6 sts. [K5, ssk, turn. P6, turn] 5 times, k5, ssk. Do *not* turn.

RS RECTANGLES
**Pick-up row (RS) Pick up and k 6 sts along side of next rectangle. Turn. P6, turn.
[K5, ssk, turn. P6, turn] 5 times, k5, ssk. Do *not* turn.
Rep from ** once more (3 RS Rectangles).
Next row (RS) Pick up and k 6 sts along side of last rectangle. Turn.
Work in St st for 12 rows. Turn (4 RS Rectangles made).

WS RECTANGLES
Next row (WS) Cast on 6 sts. Do *not* turn.
[P5, p2tog, turn. K6, turn] 5 times. P5, p2tog. Do *not* turn (WS Rectangle made).
+Pick-up row (WS) Pick up and p 6 sts along side of next

rectangle, turn. K6, turn.
[P5, p2tog, turn. K6, turn] 5
times. P5, p2tog. Do *not* turn.+
Rep from + to + across row,
working 4 WS Rectangles. Do *not*
turn. End with a WS Rectangle.
Pick–up row (WS) Pick up and
p 6 sts down side of last
rectangle, turn.
Work in St st for 12 rows. End
WS Rectangle made (5 WS
Rectangles).

RS RECTANGLES
Next row (RS) Cast on 6 sts.
Do *not* turn.
[K5, ssk, turn. P6, turn] 5 times,
k5, ssk. Do *not* turn.

++Pick–up row (RS) Pick up
and k 6 sts along side of next
rectangle. Turn. P6, turn.
[K5, ssk, turn. P6, turn] 5 times,
k5, ssk. Do *not* turn.**++**
Rep from **++** until 5 RS
Rectangles are made. Do
not turn.
Pick–up row (RS) Pick up and k
6 sts along side of last rectangle.
Turn.
Work in St st for 12 rows. Turn.

WS RECTANGLES
Next row (WS) Cast on 6 sts. Do
not turn.
Work 1 row of WS Rectangles as
before (6 WS Rectangles

worked). Do *not* turn.
Next row (WS) Pick up and p 6
sts along side of last rectangle,
turn.
Work in St st for 12 rows.
End with completed WS
Rectangle.
Cont as establlished, foll
diagram, until 15 rectangles
have been made.

LAST ROW OF TRIANGLES
With RS facing, cast on 6 sts.
*K5, ssk, turn. P4, p2tog, turn.
K4, ssk, turn. P3, p2tog, turn.
K3, ssk, turn. P2, p2tog, turn.
K2, ssk, turn. P1, p2tog, turn.
K1, ssk, turn. P2tog, turn.

Ssk. Do *not* turn. 1 st on needle.
Next row (RS) Pick up and k 5
sts, turn. P6, turn.
Rep from * to last rectangle.
Next row (RS) Pick up and k 5
sts, turn. P4, p2tog, turn.
Next row (RS) K5, turn. P3,
p2tog, turn.
Next row (RS) K4, turn. P2,
p2tog, turn.
Next row (RS) K3, turn. P1,
p2tog, turn.
Next row (RS) K2, turn. P2tog.
Fasten off.
Sew button on one corner of
kerchief and make a button loop
on opposite corner.❖

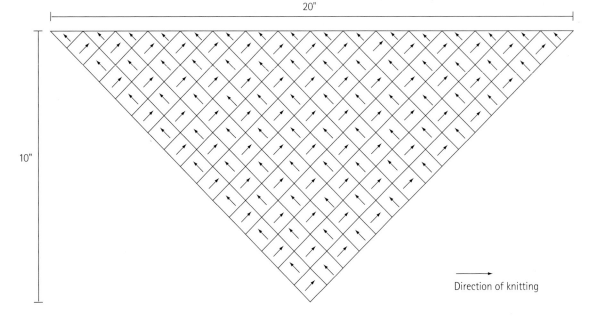

Direction of knitting

EASY

jolie jabot

You'll be pretty in pink in this face-flattering neck wrap. The simple stockinette stitch pattern is dressed up when you knit it in two shades of variegated yarn.

SIZE
Sized for adult woman.

FINISHED MEASUREMENTS
8½" x 32"/21.5cm x 81.5cm

MATERIALS
■ 2 1¾oz/50g skeins
(each approx 185yd/169m)
each of Koigu *Mori* (wool/silk) in
#m 107b dark (A) and
#m 210 light (B) **①**

■ One pair size 4 (3.5mm)
needles OR SIZE TO
OBTAIN GAUGE

GAUGE
2 Base Triangles and 1½
RS Rectangles = 4"/10cm
(after blocking)

TAKE TIME TO CHECK GAUGE.

JABOT
With A, cast on 40 sts
(multiple of 10 sts).

BASE TRIANGLES
*Row 1 (WS) P2, turn.
Row 2 (RS) K2, turn.
Row 3 P3, turn.
Row 4 K3, turn.
Row 5 P4, turn.
Row 6 K4, turn.
Row 7 P5, turn.

Row 8 K5, turn.
Row 9 P6, turn.
Row 10 K6, turn.
Row 11 P7, turn.
Row 12 K7, turn.
Row 13 P8, turn.
Row 14 K8, turn.
Row 15 P9, turn.
Row 16 K9, turn.
Row 17 P10, do *not* turn.
Rep from * for 3 more triangles—4
Base Triangles made. Turn.

RH CORNER TRIANGLE
Change to B.
Row 1 (RS) K2, turn.
Row 2 (WS) P2, turn.
Row 3 Inc in first st by knitting
into front and back of st, ssk, turn.
Row 4 P3, turn.
Row 5 Inc in first st, k1, ssk, turn.
Row 6 P4, turn.
Row 7 Inc in first st, k2, ssk, turn.
Row 8 P5, turn.
Row 9 Inc in first st, k3, ssk, turn.
Row 10 P6, turn.
Row 11 Inc in first st, k4, ssk, turn.
Row 12 P7, turn.
Row 13 Inc in first st, k5, ssk, turn.
Row 14 P8, turn.
Row 15 Inc in first st, k6, ssk, turn.
Row 16 P9, turn.
Row 17 Inc in first st, k7, ssk,

do *not* turn.
The RH Corner Triangle is
complete. Leave 10 sts on RH
needle.

RS RECTANGLES
*Pick-up row (RS) Pick up and
k 10 sts evenly along edge of next
triangle/rectangle, turn.
Row 1 (WS) P10, turn.
Row 2 K9, ssk (with last st of
rectangle and first st of next
triangle/rectangle), turn.
Rows 3–20 Rep rows 1 and 2
nine times. Do *not* turn at
end of last row. Rep from * across
row—4 RS Rectangles have
been made.

LH CORNER TRIANGLE
Pick-up row (RS) Pick up and k
10 sts along edge of last
triangle/rectangle, turn.
Row 1 P2tog, p8, turn.
Row 2 K9, turn.
Row 3 P2tog, p7, turn.
Row 4 K8, turn.
Row 5 P2tog, p6, turn.
Row 6 K7, turn.
Row 7 P2tog, p5, turn.
Row 8 K6, turn.
Row 9 P2tog, p4, turn.
Row 10 K5, turn.

Row 11 P2tog, p3, turn.
Row 12 K4, turn.
Row 13 P2tog, p2, turn.
Row 14 K3, turn.
Row 15 P2tog, p1, turn.
Row 16 K2, turn.
Row 17 P2tog, do *not* turn—1 st
remains on RH needle.

WS RECTANGLES
Change to A.
Pick-up row (WS) Pick up and
p 9 sts evenly along edge of
triangle just worked—10 sts on RH
needle, turn.
*Row 1 K10, turn.
Row 2 P8, p2tog (with last st of
rectangle and first st of next
triangle/rectangle), turn.
Rows 3–20 Rep rows 1 and 2
nine times. Do *not* turn.
Next row (WS) Pick up and
p 10 sts evenly along edge of next
RS Rectangle.
Rep from * across row—4
WS Rectangles made. Turn.
**Change to B and cont in stripe
pat as established until piece
measures approx 31"/79cm from
beg (a total of 12 rows of RS Rectangles), ending with a LH Corner
Triangle completed—1 st remains
on RH needle. Do *not* turn.

END TRIANGLES

Change to A.

*Pick-up row (WS) Pick up and p 9 sts evenly along edge of triangle just worked—10 sts on RH needle. Turn.

Row 1 (RS) K10, turn.

Row 2 P2tog, p7, p2tog, turn.

Row 3 K9, turn.

Row 4 P2tog, p6, p2tog, turn.

Row 5 K8, turn.

Row 6 P2tog, p5, p2tog, turn.

Row 7 K7, turn.

Row 8 P2tog, p4, p2tog, turn.

Row 9 K6, turn.

Row 10 P2tog, p3, p2tog, turn.

Row 11 K5, turn.

Row 12 P2tog, p2, p2tog, turn.

Row 13 K4, turn.

Row 14 P2tog, p1, p2tog, turn.

Row 15 K3, turn.

Row 16 P2tog, p2tog, turn.

Row 17 K2, turn.

Row 18 P2tog, p2tog, pass first st over 2nd st—1 st remains on RH needle.

Rep from * across row, picking up sts along edge of rectangle instead of triangle. Fasten off.

FINISHING

Block to measurements. ❖

entre nous

You can make a longer, narrower scarf by casting on 20 sts and adding additional rows of RS and WS Rectangles.

EXPERIENCED

shades of gray vest

Theresa Schabes's vest is a must-have for any fall wardrobe. Three shades of gray accented with black give it a classic look.

◆

SIZE
Sized for Woman's Small (Medium, Large).
Shown in size Small.

FINISHED MEASUREMENTS
Bust 34 (38, 42)"/86.5 (96.5, 106.5)cm

Length 25"/63.5cm

MATERIALS
■ 4 (5, 6) 1¾oz/50g skeins (each approx 164yd/149m) of Classic Elite Yarns *Fresco* (wool/alpaca/angora) in #5377 charcoal black (MC) **2**

■ 1 skein each in #5313 onyx (A) and #5303 cinder (B)

■ 1 (1, 2) skeins in #5375 graystone (C)

■ One pair each sizes 4 and 5 (3.5 and 3.75mm) needles OR SIZE TO OBTAIN GAUGE

■ Size 5 (3.75mm) circular needle, 40"/100cm long

■ Stitch markers

■ Seven ⅝"/16mm buttons

GAUGES
■ 25 sts and 36 rows = 4"/10cm over St st, using size 5 (3.75mm) needles.

■ 27 sts and 36 rows = 4"/10cm over Farrow Rib (stretched slightly), using size 5 (3.75mm) needles.
TAKE TIME TO CHECK GAUGES.

COLOR SEQUENCE FOR ENTRELAC TIERS
Work 1 tier each with *A, MC, C, B, C, and MC; rep from * for color sequence. Cut yarn after each tier has been completed, then join new color for next tier.

LEFT FRONT
TIER 1 BASE TRIANGLES
With larger needles and A, cast on 30 (33, 36) sts (a multiple of

stitch

FARROW RIB
(over a multiple of 3 sts)
Row 1 (RS) *K2, p1; rep from *, end k3.
Row 2 (WS) Rep row 1. Rep rows 1 and 2 for farrow rib.

10 (11, 12) sts).
***Row 1 (RS)** K2, turn.
Row 2 (WS) P2, turn.
Row 3 K3, turn.
Row 4 P3, turn.
Row 5 K4, turn.
Row 6 P4, turn.
Row 7 K5, turn.
Row 8 P5, turn.
Cont to work 1 more st every RS row until last row worked is:
Row 17 (19, 21) K10 (11, 12), do *not* turn.
Rep from * for 2 more triangles—3 Base Triangles made. Cut A. Turn.

TIER 2 WS RECTANGLES (WITH CORNER CAST-ON)
Join MC, cast on 10 (11, 12) sts onto LH needle.
Next row (WS) P10 (11, 12), sl last st purled to LH needle and p2tog, turn.
***Row 1 (RS)** K10 (11, 12), turn.
Row 2 P9 (10, 11), p2tog, turn.
Rows 3–18 (20, 22) Rep last 2 rows 8 (9, 10) times. Do *not* turn.
Pick-up row (WS) Pick up and p 10 (11, 12) sts evenly along next triangle, sl last picked-up st to LH needle and p2tog, turn.
Rep from * for 1 more rectangle,

then rep rows 1–18 (20, 22) once more—3 WS Rectangles made.

RH CORNER TRIANGLE (WS)
Pick-up row (WS) Pick up and p 9 (10, 11) sts evenly along edge of last triangle/rectangle, turn.
Row 1 (RS) K9 (10, 11), turn.
Row 2 P7 (8, 9), p2tog, turn.
Row 3 K8 (9, 10), turn.
Row 4 P6 (7, 8), p2tog, turn.
Row 5 K7 (8, 9), turn.
Row 6 P5 (6, 7), p2tog, turn.
Cont to dec 1 st at end of every WS row until 1 st remains. Turn.

TIER 3 RS RECTANGLES
Pick-up row (RS) With C, pick up and k 9 (10, 11) sts evenly along edge of triangle/ rectangle—10 (11, 12) sts on RH needle, k1 from LH needle and pass last picked-up st over k1, turn.
***Row 1 (WS)** P10 (11, 12), turn.
Row 2 K9 (10, 11), ssk, turn.
Rows 3–18 (20, 22) Rep last 2 rows 8 (9, 10) times. Do *not* turn.
Pick-up row (RS) Pick up and k 10 (11, 12) sts evenly along edge of next rectangle. Rep from * for 1 more rectangle, then rep rows 1–18 (20, 22) once more—3 RS Rectangles made.

entre nous

The designer chose the ribbed pattern on the back to give this vest a tailored look without a great deal of shaping.

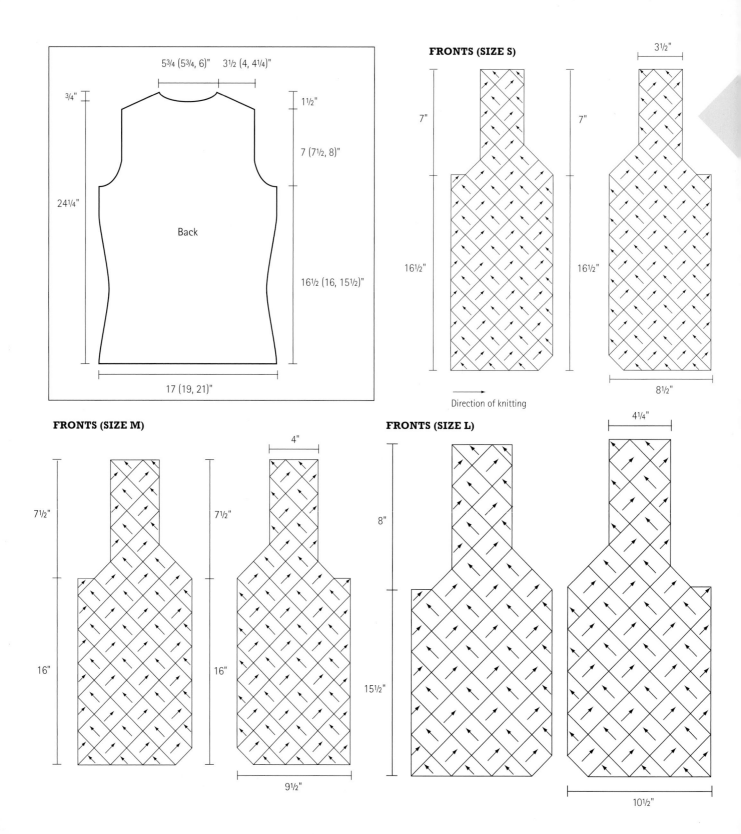

5¾ (5¾, 6)"   3½ (4, 4¼)"

¾"

24¼"

Back

1½"

7 (7½, 8)"

16½ (16, 15½)"

17 (19, 21)"

FRONTS (SIZE S)

3½"

7"

16½"

7"

16½"

8½"

→
Direction of knitting

FRONTS (SIZE M)

4"

7½"

7½"

16"

16"

9½"

FRONTS (SIZE L)

4¼"

8"

15½"

10½"

LH CORNER TRIANGLE (RS)

Pick-up row (RS) Pick up and k 9 (10, 11) sts evenly along edge of last rectangle, turn.

Row 1 (WS) P9 (10, 11), turn.
Row 2 (RS) K7 (8, 9), ssk, turn.
Row 3 P8 (9, 10), turn.
Row 4 K6 (7, 8), ssk, turn.
Row 5 P7 (8, 9), turn.
Row 6 K5 (6, 7), ssk, turn.
Cont to dec 1 st at end of every RS row until 1 st remains. Turn.

TIER 4 WS RECTANGLES

Pick-up row (WS) With B, pick up and p 9 (10, 11) sts evenly along edge of triangle—10 (11, 12) sts on RH needle, sl last picked-up st to LH needle and p2tog, turn.
***Row 1 (RS)** K10 (11, 12), turn.
Row 2 P9 (10, 11), p2tog, turn.
Rows 3–18 (20, 22) Rep last 2 rows 8 (9, 10) times. Do *not* turn.
Pick-up row (WS) Pick up and p 10 (11, 12) sts evenly along edge of rectangle.
Rep from * for 1 more rectangle, then rep rows 1–18 (20, 22) once more—3 WS Rectangles made.

Work 1 RH Triangle (WS).

TIER 5 Rep Tier 3.

TIER 6 With MC, rep Tier 4.

TIERS 7–13 (11, 9) Cont in color sequence as established, [rep Tiers 3 and 4] 3 (2, 1) times more, then rep Tier 3 once more.

SHAPE NECK AND ARMHOLE
TIER 14 (12, 10)

Work 3 WS Rectangles as for Tier 4 (on last WS row of 3rd rectangle, bind off all sts as you go)—1 st remains after bind-off.

LEFT UNDERARM WEDGE (WS)

***Pick-up row (WS)** Pick up and p 8 (9, 10) sts evenly along edge of last rectangle—9 (10, 11) sts on RH needle, turn.
Row 1 (RS) K to end, turn.
Row 2 (WS) P2tog, p to last 2 sts, ssp, turn.
Rep last 2 rows until 3 (2, 3) sts remain.
Next row (RS) K3tog (k2tog, k3tog). Fasten off.

TIER 15 (13, 11)

Pick-up row (RS) Beg at tip of last WS Rectangle, pick up and k 10 (11, 12) sts evenly along edge of rectangle, k1 from LH needle and pass last picked-up st over k1, turn.
Row 1 (WS) P10 (11, 12), turn.
Row 2 K9 (10, 11), ssk, turn.
Rows 3–18 (20, 22) Rep last 2 rows 8 (9, 10) times. Do *not* turn.
Work 1 more RS Rectangle—2 RS Rectangles made.
Next row (WS) Bind off 9 (10, 11) sts—1 st remains. Do *not* turn.

TIERS 16, 18 & 20
(14, 16 & 18; 12, 14 & 16)

Work 1 WS Rectangle and 1 RH Triangle (WS).

TIERS 17 & 19
(15 & 17; 13 & 15)
Work 1 RS Rectangle and 1 LH Triangle (RS).

TIER 21 (19, 17)
TOP TRIANGLE

Pick-up row (RS) Pick up and k 9 (10, 11) sts evenly along edge of triangle—10 (11, 12) sts on RH needle, k1 from LH needle and pass last picked-up st over k1, turn.
Row 1 (WS) P to end, turn.
Row 2 (RS) Ssk, k to last st of triangle, ssk, turn.
Rows 3–14 (16, 18) Rep last 2 rows 6 (7, 8) times.
Row 15 (17, 19) P3, turn.
Row 16 (18, 20) [Ssk] twice, turn.
Row 17 (19, 21) P2, turn.
Row 18 (20, 22) SK2P, do *not* turn—1 st remains.

HALF TRIANGLE
(LEFT CORNER) (RS)

***Pick-up row (RS)** Pick up and k 8 (9, 10) sts evenly along edge of last rectangle—9 (10 11) sts on RH needle, turn.
Row 1 (WS) P to end, turn.
Row 2 (RS) Ssk, k to last 2 sts, k2tog, turn.
Rep last 2 rows until 3 (2, 3) sts remain.
Next row (WS) P3tog (p2tog, p3tog). Fasten off.

RIGHT FRONT
TIER 1
BASE TRIANGLES
Work as for Left Front.

TIER 2
LH TRIANGLE (WS)
Row 1 (WS) P1fb, p2tog, turn.
Row 2 (RS) K3, turn.
Row 3 P1fb, p1, p2tog, turn.
Row 4 K4, turn.
Row 5 P1fb, p2, p2tog, turn.
Row 6 K5, turn.
Cont to work 1 more st after the p1fb on every WS row until last row worked is:
Row 15 (17, 19) P1fb, p7 (8, 9), p2tog. Do *not* turn.

Work 3 WS Rectangles. Turn.

TIER 3
RH TRIANGLE (RS)
Row 1 (RS) K1fb, ssk, turn.
Row 2 (RS) P3, turn.
Row 3 K1fb, k1, ssk, turn.
Row 4 P4, turn.
Row 5 K1fb, k2, ssk, turn.
Row 6 P5, turn.
Cont to work 1 more st after the k1fb on every RS row until last row worked is:
Row 15 (17, 19) K1fb, k7 (8, 9), ssk. Do *not* turn.

TIERS 4–13 (11, 9)
Cont in color sequence as established, [rep Tiers 2 and 3] 5 (4, 3) times more.

SHAPE NECK AND ARMHOLE

TIER 14 (12, 10)
RIGHT UNDERARM WEDGE (WS)

Row 1 (WS) P1fb, p2tog, turn.
Row 2 (RS) K3, turn.
Row 3 P1fb, p1, p2tog, turn.
Row 4 K4, turn.
Row 5 P1fb, p2, p2tog, turn.
Row 6 K5, turn.
Row 7 P1fb, p3, p2tog, turn.
Row 8 K6, turn.
Size L only: Row 9 P1fb, p4, p2tog, turn.
Row 10 K7, turn.
Row 11 P2tog, p4, p2tog, turn.
Row 12 K6, turn.
All Sizes: Row 9 (9, 13) P2tog, p3, p2tog, turn.
Row 10 (10, 14) K5, turn.
Row 11 (11, 15) P2tog, p2, p2tog, turn.
Row 12 (12, 16) K4, turn.
Row 13 (13, 17) P2tog, p1, p2tog, turn.
Row 14 (14, 18) K3, turn.
Row 15 (15, 19) [P2tog] twice, turn.
Row 16 (16, 20) K2, turn.
Row 17 (17, 21) P2tog (p3tog, p2tog)—1 st remains. Do *not* turn.

Work 3 WS Rectangles. Turn. Bind off 9 (10, 11) sts—1 st remains.

TIER 15 (13, 11)
Work 2 RS Rectangles.

TIERS 16, 18 & 20 (14, 16 & 18; 12, 14 & 16)
Work 1 LH Triangle (WS) and 1 WS Rectangle.

TIERS 17 & 19 (15 & 17; 13 & 15)
Work 1 RH Triangle (RS) and 1 RS Rectangle.

TIER 21 (19, 17)
HALF TRIANGLE (RIGHT CORNER) (RS)

Row 1 (RS) K1fb, ssk, turn.
Row 2 (WS) P3, turn.
Row 3 K1fb, k1, ssk, turn.
Row 4 P4, turn.
Row 5 K1fb, k2, ssk, turn.
Row 6 P5, turn.
Row 7 K1fb, k3, ssk, turn.
Row 8 P6, turn.
Size L only: Row 9 K1fb, k4, ssk, turn.
Row 10 P7, turn.
Row 11 Ssk, k4, ssk, turn.
Row 12 P6, turn.
All Sizes: Row 9 (9, 13) Ssk, k3, ssk, turn.
Row 10 (10, 14) P5, turn.
Row 11 (11, 15) Ssk, k2, ssk, turn.
Row 12 (12, 16) P4, turn.
Row 13 (13, 17) Ssk, k1, ssk, turn.
Row 14 (14, 18) P3, turn.
Row 15 (15, 19) [Ssk] twice, turn.
Row 16 (16, 20) P2, turn.
Row 17 (17, 21) Ssk (SK2P, ssk)—1 st remains. Do *not* turn.

Work 1 End Triangle.
Fasten off.

BACK

With larger needles and MC, cast on 117 (129, 141) sts. Work in farrow rib until piece measures 9"/23cm from beg.

WAIST SHAPING

Change to smaller needles and work for 3"/7.5cm.
Change to larger needles and work even until piece measures 16½ (16, 15½)"/42 (40.5, 39.5)cm from beg, end with a WS row.

ARMHOLE SHAPING

Bind off 6 (8, 9) sts at beg of next 2 rows, then 2 sts at beg of next 6 rows. Dec 1 st each side every RS row 3 (3, 6) times—87 (95, 99) sts. Work even until armhole measures 7 (7½, 8)"/18 (19, 20.5)cm, end with a WS row.

SHOULDER AND NECK SHAPING

Bind off 4 sts at beg of next 6 (14, 12) rows, 3 (0, 5) sts at beg of next 8 (0, 2) rows, AT SAME TIME, after 6 rows of shoulder shaping have been worked and armhole measures approx 7¾ (8¼, 8¾)"/19.5 (21, 22)cm, join 2nd ball of yarn, bind off center 11 (11, 13) sts for neck and, working both sides at same time, bind off from each neck edge 6 (8, 8) sts once, 5 sts 1 (0, 0) time, and 3 sts 1 (2, 2) times.

FINISHING

Block pieces. Sew shoulder seams.

ARMHOLE BANDS

With RS facing, larger needles and MC, pick up and k 108 (118, 128) sts evenly around armhole edge.
Rows 1 and 3 (WS) Knit.
Row 2 Purl.
Bind off.

FRONT AND NECK BAND

Place 7 markers along Right Front edge for buttonholes, with the first at tip of first WS Rectangle at lower edge, the last at tip of WS Rectangle at beg of neck shaping, and 5 others spaced evenly between. With RS facing, circular needle and MC, beginning at side edge of Right Front, pick up and k36 (40, 44) sts evenly along straight portion of lower edge, 155 sts along Right Front edge to shoulder, working buttonholes by casting on 2 sts at each marker (include these sts in st count) and skipping ½"/1.5cm before resuming picking up sts, 45 (45, 47) sts along back neck, 155 sts along Left Front edge and 36 (40, 44) sts along straight edge to side edge—427 (435, 445) sts. Work as for Armhole Bands. Sew side seams, including Armhole Bands. Sew on buttons. ❖

EXPERIENCED

felted shoulder bag

Felted entrelac creates the look of traditional intarsia knitting, but without the hassle of carrying colors. One side is a zigzag pattern, while the other is argyle.

FINISHED MEASUREMENTS
20"/50.5cm wide (after felting)
14"/35.5cm tall (after felting)

MATERIALS
■ 3 3½oz/100g balls (each approx 220yd/200m) of Nashua Handknits *Creative Focus Worsted* (wool/alpaca) in #2124 cordovan (A) ■

■ 2 balls in #3249 chocolate (B)

■ 1 ball in #0282 taupe heather (C)

■ 1 pair size 10 (6mm) needles OR SIZE TO OBTAIN GAUGE

■ 1 pair size 13 (9mm) needles for bind off

GAUGE
■ 13 sts and 20 rows = 4"/10cm over St st (before felting).
TAKE TIME TO CHECK GAUGE.

FRONT
With size 10 (6mm) needles and A, cast on 60 sts (multiple of 10). Work 19 rows in St st for base, ending with a RS row.

BASE TRIANGLES
*Row 1 (WS) P2, turn.
Row 2 (RS) K2, turn.
Row 3 P3, turn.
Row 4 K3, turn.
Row 5 P4, turn.
Row 6 K4, turn.
Row 7 P5, turn.
Row 8 K5, turn.
Row 9 P6, turn.
Row 10 K6, turn.
Row 11 P7, turn.
Row 12 K7, turn.
Row 13 P8, turn.
Row 14 K8, turn.
Row 15 P9, turn.
Row 16 K9, turn.
Row 17 P10, do *not* turn.
Rep from * for 5 more triangles—6 Base Triangles made. Turn.

RH CORNER TRIANGLE
Change to B.
Row 1 (RS) K2, turn.

Row 2 (WS) P2, turn.
Row 3 Inc in first st by knitting into front and back of st, ssk, turn.
Row 4 P3, turn.
Row 5 Inc in first st, k1, ssk, turn.
Row 6 P4, turn.
Row 7 Inc in first st, k2, ssk, turn.
Row 8 P5, turn.
Row 9 Inc in first st, k3, ssk, turn.
Row 10 P6, turn.
Row 11 Inc in first st, k4, ssk, turn.
Row 12 P7, turn.
Row 13 Inc in first st, k5, ssk, turn.
Row 14 P8, turn.
Row 15 Inc in first st, k6, ssk, turn.
Row 16 P9, turn.
Row 17 Inc in first st, k7, ssk, do *not* turn.
The RH Corner Triangle is complete. Leave 10 sts on RH needle.

RS RECTANGLES
*Pick-up row (RS) Pick up and k 10 sts evenly along edge of next triangle/rectangle, turn.
Row 1 (WS) P10, turn.
Row 2 K9, ssk (with last st of

rectangle and first st of next triangle/rectangle), turn.
Rows 3–20 Rep rows 1 and 2 nine times. Do *not* turn at end of last row.
Rep from * across row—5 RS Rectangles made.

LH CORNER TRIANGLE
Pick-up row (RS)

Pick up and k 10 sts along edge of last triangle/rectangle, turn.
Row 1 P2tog, p8, turn.
Row 2 K9, turn.
Row 3 P2tog, p7, turn.
Row 4 K8, turn.
Row 5 P2tog, p6, turn.
Row 6 K7, turn.
Row 7 P2tog, p5, turn.
Row 8 K6, turn.
Row 9 P2tog, p4, turn.
Row 10 K5, turn.
Row 11 P2tog, p3, turn.
Row 12 K4, turn.
Row 13 P2tog, p2, turn.
Row 14 K3, turn.
Row 15 P2tog, p1, turn.
Row 16 K2, turn.
Row 17 P2tog, do *not* turn—1 st remains on RH needle.

DIAGRAM 1 (ZIGZAG)

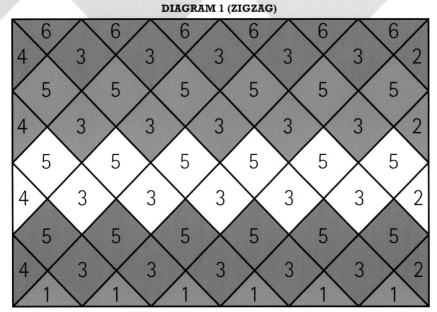

Placement Key

1 Base Triangle

2 RH Corner Triangle

3 RS Rectangle

4 LH Corner Triangle

5 WS Rectangle

6 End Triangle

DIAGRAM 2 (ARGYLE)

Color Key

■ Cordovan (A)

■ Chocolate (B)

□ Taupe heather (C)

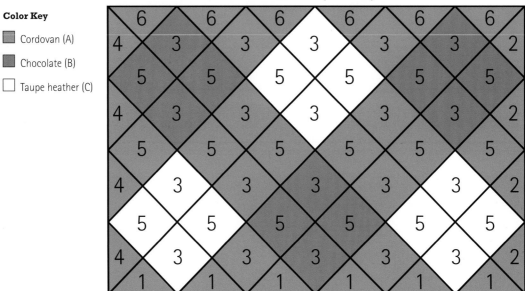

WS RECTANGLES

Pick-up row (WS) Pick up and p 9 sts evenly along edge of triangle just worked—10 sts on RH needle, turn.

*Row 1 K10, turn.

Row 2 P9, p2tog (with last st of rectangle and first st of next triangle/rectangle), turn.

Rows 3–20 Rep rows 1 and 2 nine times. Do *not* turn.

Next row (WS) Pick up and p 10 sts evenly along edge of next RS Rectangle.

Rep from * across row—6 WS Rectangles made. Turn.

Continue following diagram 1 for color placement until 4 rows of RS Triangles made. End with a LH Corner Triangle completed.

END TRIANGLES

Work End Triangles in B as foll:

SHORT ROWS

Next row (WS) Pick up and p 9 sts along edge of triangle just worked. Turn.

*Next row (RS) K10, turn.

Next row (WS) P9, p2 tog (1 from triangle), turn.

Next row K9 (leaving 1 st on needle), turn.

Next row P8, p2tog, turn.

Next row K8, turn.

Next row P7, p2tog, turn.

Next row K7, turn.

Next row P6, p2tog, turn.

Next row K6, turn.

Next row P5, p2tog, turn.

Next row K5, turn.

Next row P4, p2tog, turn.

Next row K4, turn.

Next row P3, p2tog, turn.

Next row K3, turn.

Next row P2, p2tog, turn.

Next row K2, turn.

Next row P1, p2tog, turn.

Next row K1, turn.

Next row P2tog. Do *not* turn, 10 sts on RH needle.

Pick up and p 10 sts along next rectangle and repeat from * across row—60 sts.

Next row (RS) K60.

Next row P60.

Bind off *loosely* with size 13 (9mm) needle.

BACK

With RS facing and A and size 10 (6mm) needle, pick up and k 60 sts evenly along cast-on edge of stockinette section of front. Work as for front, skipping St st rows and beg with 6 Base Triangles and following diagram 2 for color placement. Work last 2 rows in A—60 sts.

Bind off with size 13 (9mm) needle.

SIDES

With RS facing and A and size 10 (6mm) needle, pick up and k 20 sts along base sides. Work in St st until same height as front. Bind off.

Repeat for 2nd side.

STRAP

With A and size 10 (6mm) needles, cast on 10 sts and work in garter st (knit every row) for 60"/152cm. Bind off.

Sew front and back of bag to side pieces.

Do *not* sew on strap.

FINISHING

FELTING

Place bag and strap in washing machine set to hot wash/cold rinse with low water level. Add a pair of jeans for abrasion and balanced agitation. Add 1 tablespoon dishwashing detergent and ¼ cup baking soda at beginning of wash cycle. Rep cycle, if necessary, until pieces are felted to desired size. Let air dry and block piece flat.

Cut strap in half and sew onto bag 6"/15cm from each side (see photo). ❖

BACK

entre nous

To be sure that the yarns you choose are colorfast, make a swatch (not necessarily in entrelac) using the three colors and felt it before beginning the project.

INTERMEDIATE

triangle throw

Brian Kohler's pattern does double duty: Make it small to wear as a cozy wrap; cast on more stitches to create a luxurious blanket.

◆

SIZE
Sized for Shawl (Blanket). Shown as Blanket.

FINISHED MEASUREMENTS
Approx 84" x 42" (132" x 66")/ 213.5cm x 106.5cm (335cm x 167.5cm)

MATERIALS
■ 4 (7) 3½oz/100g balls (each approx 164yd/150m) of Skacel *Pur Schoppel* (wool) each in #1507 (A), #1914 (B) and #1659 (C) ④

■ Size 8 (5mm) circular needle, 40 (47–60)"/100 (120–153)cm long, OR SIZE TO OBTAIN GAUGE

■ Two size 8 (5mm) double-pointed needles (dpns)

GAUGE
16 sts and 24 rows = 4"/10cm over St st using size 8 (5mm) needle.
TAKE TIME TO CHECK GAUGE.

SHAWL (BLANKET)
BASE TRIANGLES
With A, cast on 224 (352) sts (a multiple of 8 sts).
*Row 1 (RS) K1, turn.
Row 2 (WS) P1, turn.
Row 3 Sl 1, k1, turn.
Row 4 P2, turn.
Row 5 Sl 1, k2, turn.
Row 6 P3, turn.
Row 7 Sl 1, k3, turn.
Row 8 P4, turn.
Row 9 Sl 1, k4, turn.
Row 10 P5, turn.
Row 11 Sl 1, k5, turn.
Row 12 P6, turn.
Row 13 Sl 1, k6, turn.
Row 14 P7, turn.
Row 15 Sl 1, k7, do *not* turn.

note
Sl sts purlwise with yarn in back on RS rows, and with yarn in front on WS rows.

Rep from * for 26 (42) more Base Triangles. Work rows 1–14 once more.
Next row (RS) Bind off 8 sts—28 (44) Base Triangles made. Turn.

WS RECTANGLES
*Pick-up row (WS) With B, pick up and p 8 sts evenly along sl st edge of triangle/rectangle, sl last picked-up st to LH needle and p2tog (with last st of rectangle and first st of next triangle/rectangle), turn.
Row 1 (RS) K8, turn.
Row 2 Sl 1, p6, p2tog, turn.
Rows 3–14 Rep rows 1 and 2 six times. Do *not* turn.
Rep from * for 25 (41) more rectangles. Work rows 1–14 once more, binding off sts of row 14 as you go—27 (43) WS Rectangles made. Turn.

RS RECTANGLES
*Pick-up row (RS) With C, pick up and k 8 sts evenly along sl st edge of rectangle, sl last picked-up st to LH needle and ssk, turn.
Row 1 (WS) P8, turn.

Row 2 Sl 1, k6, ssk, turn.
Rows 3–14 Rep rows 1 and 2 six times. Do *not* turn.
Rep from * for 24 (40) more rectangles. Work rows 1–14 once more, binding off sts of row 14 as you go—26 (42) RS Rectangles made. Turn.

**Work 25 (41) WS Rectangles. Work 24 (40) RS Rectangles. Rep from **, working 1 less rectangle each time, and working each row of rectangles with a new color.

FINISHING
I-CORD FRINGE
With dpn, cast on 4 sts.
Row 1 K4, do *not* turn. Slide sts to other end of needle. Rep row 1 until cord measures 5"/12.5cm. Bind off. Make a cord for every intersection of rows on each side of piece and attach cord at intersection. Tie a knot in end of each cord. ❖

INTERMEDIATE

scarf set

Knit up a trio of neck-warming scarves. The bobble and leaf lace scarves feature allover entrelac patterns, while the striped scarf is just bordered with entrelac.

Bobble Scarf

FINISHED MEASUREMENTS

7" X 62"/17.5cm X 157.5cm

MATERIALS

■ 3 3½oz/100g skeins (each approx 130yd/120m) of Tahki Yarns/Tahki•Stacy Charles, Inc. *Montana* (wool) in #001 natural (6)

■ One pair size 13 (9mm) knitting needles OR SIZE TO OBTAIN GAUGE

GAUGE

10 sts and 14 rows = 4"/10cm over St st.
TAKE TIME TO CHECK GAUGE.

SCARF

Cast on 15 sts (multiple of 5 sts).

BASE TRIANGLES

*Row 1 (WS) P2, turn.
Row 2 (RS) K2, turn.
Row 3 P3, turn.
Row 4 K1, MB, k1, turn.
Row 5 P4, turn.
Row 6 K4, turn.
Row 7 P5, do *not* turn.
Rep from * for two more triangles—3 triangles made. Turn.

RH CORNER TRIANGLE

Row 1 (RS) K2, turn.
Row 2 P2, turn.
Row 3 Inc in first st by knitting into front and back of st, ssk, turn.
Row 4 P3, turn.
Row 5 Inc in first st, MB, ssk, turn.
Row 6 P4, turn.
Row 7 Inc in first st, k2, ssk, do *not* turn.
The RH Corner Triangle is complete. Leave sts on RH needle.

RS RECTANGLES

*Pick-up row (RS) Pick up and k 5 sts evenly along edge of next triangle/rectangle, turn.
Row 1 P5, turn.
Row 2 K4, ssk (with last st of rectangle and first st of next triangle/rectangle), turn.
Row 3 P5, turn.
Row 4 K2, MB, k1, ssk, turn.
Row 5 P5, turn.
Row 6 K4, ssk, turn.
Row 7 P5, turn.
Row 8 K4, ssk, turn.
Row 9 P5, turn.
Row 10 K4, ssk, do *not* turn.

stitch

MAKE BOBBLE (MB)

(K1, p1, k1) in next st to make 3 sts in 1, turn. P3, turn. Slip 1, k2tog, pass slipped st over—1 st rem on needle.

Rep from * across row—2 RS Rectangles made.

LH CORNER TRIANGLE

Pick-up row (RS) Pick up and k 5 sts along edge of last triangle/rectangle, turn.
Row 1 P2tog, p3, turn.
Row 2 K4, turn.
Row 3 P2tog, p2, turn.
Row 4 K1, MB, k1, turn.
Row 5 P2tog, p1, turn.
Row 6 K2, turn.
Row 7 P2tog, do *not* turn—1 st remains on needle.

WS RECTANGLES

Pick-up row (WS) Pick up and p 4 sts evenly along edge of triangle just worked—5 sts, turn.
*Row 1 K5, turn.
Row 2 P4, p2tog (with last st of rectangle and first st of next triangle/rectangle), turn.
Row 3 K5.
Row 4 P4, p2tog, turn.
Row 5 K2, MB, k2, turn.
Row 6 P4, p2tog, turn.
Row 7 K5, turn.
Row 8 P4, p2tog, turn.
Row 9 K5, turn.
Row 10 P4, p2tog, do *not* turn.
Next row (WS) Pick up and p 5 sts evenly along edge of next RS Rectangle.
Rep from * across row—3 WS Rectangles made. Turn.

Continue as established until 3 rows of RS Rectangles have been made, then work even, omitting bobbles, until 21 rows of RS Rectangles have been made. Work 1 row of WS Rectangles and continue in bobble pat until 3 rows of RS Rectangles have been made (to correspond with beginning of scarf). End with 1 LH Corner Triangle completed.

END TRIANGLES

*Pick-up row (WS) Pick up and p 4 sts evenly along edge of triangle just worked—5 sts. Turn.
Row 1 (RS) K5, turn.

From left to right:
Bobble Scarf, Striped
& Ribbed Scarf and
Leaf Lace Scarf.

Row 2 P2tog, p2, p2tog, turn.
Row 3 K4, turn.
Row 4 P2tog, p1, p2tog, turn.
Row 5 K1, MB, k1, turn.
Row 6 P2tog, p2tog, turn.
Row 7 K2, turn.
Row 8 P2tog, p2tog, pass 1st st over 2nd st—1 st remains on needle. Do *not* turn.
Rep from * across row, picking up sts along edge of rectangle instead of triangle.
Fasten off rem st. ❖

Striped & Ribbed Scarf

FINISHED MEASUREMENTS
7½" x 60"/19.5cm x 152.5cm

MATERIALS
■ 2 3½oz/100g skeins (each approx 183yd/167m) of Tahki Yarns/Tahki•Stacy Charles, Inc. *Donegal Tweed* (wool) each in #830 brown (A) and #848 cream (B) **(4)**

■ One pair size 8 (5mm) needles OR SIZE TO OBTAIN GAUGE

GAUGE
16 sts and 24 rows = 4"/10cm over garter stripe pat using size 8 (5mm) needles.
TAKE TIME TO CHECK GAUGE.

stitches

SEEDED RIB
(multiple of 4 sts plus 3)
Row 1 (RS) K1, *p1, k3; rep from *, end p1, k2.
Row 2 K1, *k3, p1; rep from *, end k3.
Rep rows 1 and 2 for seeded rib.

GARTER STRIPE
*Work 6 rows in St st with A. K 4 rows B; rep from * (10 rows) for garter stripe.

SCARF
With A, cast on 24 sts (multiple of 8 sts).

BASE TRIANGLES
*Row 1 (WS)** P2, turn.
Row 2 (RS) K2, turn.
Row 3 P3, turn.
Row 4 K3, turn.
Row 5 P4, turn.
Row 6 K4, turn.
Row 7 P5, turn.
Row 8 K5, turn.
Row 9 P6, turn.
Row 10 K6, turn.
Row 11 P7, turn.
Row 12 K7, turn.
Row 13 P8, do *not* turn.
Rep from * for two more triangles—3 Base Triangles made. Turn.

Bobble Scarf

RH CORNER TRIANGLE
Change to B.
Row 1 (RS) K2, turn.
Row 2 (WS) P2, turn.
Row 3 Inc in first st by knitting into front and back of st, ssk, turn.
Row 4 P3, turn.
Row 5 Inc in first st, k1, ssk, turn.
Row 6 P4, turn.
Row 7 Inc in first st, k2, ssk, turn.
Row 8 P5, turn.
Row 9 Inc in first st, k3, ssk, turn.

Row 10 P6, turn.
Row 11 Inc in first st, k4, ssk, turn.
Row 12 P7, turn.
Row 13 Inc in first st, k5, ssk, do *not* turn.
The RH Corner Triangle is complete. Leave 8 sts on RH needle.

RS RECTANGLES
*Pick-up row (RS)** Pick up and k 8 sts evenly along edge of next

triangle/rectangle, turn.
Row 1 (WS) K1, p1, k3, p1, k2, turn.
Row 2 K1, k3, p1, k2, ssk (with last st of rectangle and first st of next triangle/rectangle), turn.
Rows 3–16 Rep rows 1 and 2 seven times, keeping in seeded rib as established. Do *not* turn at end of last row.
Rep from * across row—2 RS Rectangles made.

LH CORNER TRIANGLE

Pick-up row (RS) Pick up and k 8 sts along edge of last triangle/rectangle, turn.
Row 1 P2tog, p6, turn.
Row 2 K7, turn.
Row 3 P2tog, p5, turn.
Row 4 K6, turn.
Row 5 P2tog, p4, turn.
Row 6 K5, turn.
Row 7 P2tog, p3, turn.
Row 8 K4, turn.
Row 9 P2tog, p2, turn.
Row 10 K3, turn.
Row 11 P2tog, p1, turn.
Row 12 K2, turn.
Row 13 P2tog, do *not* turn—1 st remains on RH needle.

WS RECTANGLES

Change to A.
Pick-up row (WS) Pick up and p 7 sts evenly along edge of triangle just worked—8 sts, turn.

*Row 1 (RS) K1, k3, p1, k3.
Row 2 K1, p1, k3, p1, k1, ssk (with last st of rectangle and first st of next triangle/rectangle), turn.
Rows 3–16 Rep rows 1 and 2 seven times, keeping in seeded rib. Do *not* turn.
Next row (WS) Pick up and p 8 sts evenly along edge of next RS rectangle. Turn.
Rep from * across row—3 WS Rectangles have been made. Turn.

Change to B and work 1 RH Corner Triangle, 1 row of RS Rectangles and 1 LH Corner Triangle.

END TRIANGLES

Change to A.
*Pick-up row (WS) Pick up and p 7 sts evenly along edge of triangle just worked—8 sts on RH needle. Turn.
Row 1 (RS) K7, wrap and turn. (see page 14).
Row 2 P6, p2tog, turn.
Row 3 K6, wrap and turn.
Row 4 P5, p2tog, turn.
Row 5 K5, wrap and turn.
Row 6 P4, p2tog, turn.
Row 7 K4, wrap and turn.
Row 8 P3, p2tog, turn.
Row 9 K3, wrap and turn.
Row 10 P2, p2tog, turn.
Row 11 K2, wrap and turn.

Row 12 P1, p2tog, turn.
Row 13 K1, wrap and turn.
Row 14 P3tog—8 sts on RH needle.
Rep from * across row, picking up 8 sts along edge of rectangle instead of 7, until all triangles are made—24 sts.
Next row (WS) Purl across, inc 6 sts evenly spaced—30 sts.

BODY OF SCARF

Work in garter stripe pat until

scarf measures 52"/132cm from beg, ending with 5 rows of St st.
Next row (RS) Knit, dec 8 sts evenly spaced across—24 sts.

END OF SCARF (WS)

Work entrelac same as beginning of scarf, beginning with Base Triangles and working End Triangles as for Leaf Lace Scarf (see page 134), picking up 7 sts instead of 8. ❖

Striped & Ribbed Scarf

Leaf Lace Scarf

FINISHED MEASUREMENTS

6" X 48"/15.5cm x 122cm

MATERIALS

■ 2 3½oz/100g skeins (each approx 220yd/200m) of Cascade Yarns *220 Heathers* (wool) in #2452 green (4)

■ One pair size 8 (5mm) knitting needles OR SIZE TO OBTAIN GAUGE

GAUGE

One Base Triangle and one RS Rectangle = 3"/7.5cm. TAKE TIME TO CHECK GAUGE.

entre nous

Knit this scarf in a lace-weight yarn, for a delicate, feminine look. You can also wear it with the wrong side facing as the pattern is equally interesting.

SCARF

Cast on 18 sts (multiple of 9 sts).

BASE TRIANGLES

*Row 1 (WS) P2, turn.
Row 2 (RS) K2, turn.
Row 3 P3, turn.
Row 4 K3, turn.
Row 5 P4, turn.
Row 6 K4, turn.
Row 7 P5, turn.
Row 8 K5, turn.
Row 9 P6, turn.
Row 10 K6, turn.
Row 11 P7, turn.
Row 12 K7, turn.
Row 13 P8, turn.
Row 14 K8, turn.
Row 15 P9, do *not* turn.
Rep from * for one more triangle—2 Base Triangles made. Turn.

RH CORNER TRIANGLE

Row 1 (RS) K2, turn.
Row 2 (WS) P2, turn.
Row 3 Inc in first st by knitting into front and back of st, ssk, turn.
Row 4 P3, turn.
Row 5 Inc in first st, k1, ssk, turn.
Row 6 P4, turn.
Row 7 Inc in first st, k2, ssk, turn.
Row 8 P5, turn.
Row 9 Inc in first st, k3, ssk, turn.
Row 10 P6, turn.
Row 11 Inc in first st, k4, ssk, turn.
Row 12 P7, turn.
Row 13 Inc in first st, k5, ssk, turn.
Row 14 P8, turn.
Row 15 Inc in first st, k6, ssk, do *not* turn.
The RH Corner Triangle is complete. Leave 9 sts on RH needle.

RS RECTANGLE

*Pick-up row (RS) Pick up and k 9 sts evenly along edge of next triangle/rectangle, turn.
Row 1 (WS) K9, turn.
Row 2 P4, yo, k1, yo, p3, p2tog (with last st of rectangle and first st of next triangle/rectangle), turn.
Row 3 K4, p3, k4, turn.
Row 4 P4, k1, yo, k1, yo, k1, p3, p2tog, turn.
Row 5 K4, p5, k4, turn.
Row 6 P4, k2, yo, k1, yo, k2, p3, p2tog, turn.
Row 7 K4, p7, k4, turn.
Row 8 P4, k3, yo, k1, yo, k3, p3, p2tog, turn.
Row 9 K4, p9, k4, turn.
Row 10 P4, ssk, k5, k2tog, p3, p2tog, turn.
Row 11 K4, p7, k4, turn.
Row 12 P4, ssk, k3, k2tog, p3, p2tog, turn.
Row 13 K4, p5, k4, turn.
Row 14 P4, ssk, k1, k2tog, p3, p2tog, turn.
Row 15 K4, p3, k4, turn.
Row 16 P4, sl 1, k2tog, psso, p3, p2tog, turn.
Row 17 K9, turn.
Row 18 P8, p2tog, do *not* turn.

LH CORNER TRIANGLE

Pick-up row (RS) Pick up and k 9 sts along edge of last triangle/rectangle, turn.
Row 1 P2tog, p7, turn.
Row 2 K8, turn.
Row 3 P2tog, p6, turn.
Row 4 K7, turn.
Row 5 P2tog, p5, turn.
Row 6 K6, turn.
Row 7 P2tog, p4, turn.
Row 8 K5, turn.
Row 9 P2tog, p3, turn.
Row 10 K4, turn.
Row 11 P2tog, p2, turn.
Row 12 K3, turn.
Row 13 P2tog, p1, turn.
Row 14 K2, turn.
Row 15 P2tog, do *not* turn—1 st remains on RH needle.

WS RECTANGLES

Pick-up row (WS) Pick up and p 8 sts evenly along edge of triangle just made—9 sts, turn.

*Row 1 (RS) P4, yo, k1, yo, p4, turn.

Row 2 K4, p3, k3, k2tog (with last st of rectangle and first st of next triangle/rectangle), turn.

Row 3 P4, k1, yo, k1, yo, k1, p4.

Row 4 K4, p5, k3, k2tog.

Row 5 P4, k2, yo, k1, yo, k2, p4.

Row 6 K4, p7, k3, k2tog.

Row 7 P4, k3, yo, k1, yo, k3, p4.

Row 8 K4, p9, k3, k2tog.

Row 9 P4, ssk, k5, k2tog, p4.

Row 10 K4, p7, k3, k2tog.

Row 11 P4, ssk, k3, k2tog, p4.

Row 12 K4, p5, k3, k2tog.

Row 13 P4, ssk, k1, k2tog, p4.

Row 14 K4, p3, k3, k2tog.

Row 15 P4, sl 1, k2tog, psso, p4.

Row 16 K8, k2tog.

Row 17 P9.

Row 18 K8, k2tog, do *not* turn.

Next row (WS) Pick up and p 9 sts evenly along edge of next RS Rectangle.

Rep from * across row—2 WS Rectangles made. Turn.

Continue as established until 16 RS Rectangles have been made, ending with 1 LH Corner Triangle completed.

END TRIANGLES

*Pick-up row (WS) Pick up and p 8 sts evenly along edge of triangle just worked—9 sts on RH needle. Turn.

Row 1 (RS) K9, turn.

Row 2 P2tog, p6, p2tog, turn.

Row 3 K8, turn.

Row 4 P2tog, p5, p2tog, turn.

Row 5 K7, turn.

Row 6 P2tog, p4, p2tog, turn.

Row 7 K6, turn.

Row 8 P2tog, p3, p2tog, turn.

Row 9 K5, turn.

Row 10 P2tog, p2, p2tog, turn.

Row 11 K4, turn.

Row 12 P2tog, p1, p2tog, turn.

Row 13 K3, turn.

Row 14 P2tog, p2tog, turn.

Row 15 K2, turn.

Row 16 P2tog, p2tog, pass 1st st over 2nd st—1 st remains on RH needle.

Rep from * across row, picking up sts along edge of rectangle instead of triangle. Fasten off.

FINISHING

Block to measurements. ❖

Leaf Lace Scarf

135

EASY

eyelet wristers

These colorful arm warmers are just an entrelac piece seamed up the side with an opening left for the thumb. They couldn't be simpler or more fun to wear.

◆

SIZE
Sized for adult woman.

FINISHED MEASUREMENTS
Width 7½"/19cm
Length 8½"/21.5cm

MATERIALS
■ 1 5½oz/155g skein (approx 350yd/315m) of Fiesta Yarns *Ballet* (superfine alpaca/tencel) in #29121 poppies (3)

■ One pair size 6 (4mm) needles OR SIZE TO OBTAIN GAUGE

GAUGE
22 sts and 28 rows = 4"/10cm over St st.
TAKE TIME TO CHECK GAUGE.

WRISTERS
Cast on 30 sts (multiple of 10 sts).

BASE TRIANGLES
*Row 1 (WS) P2, turn.
Row 2 (RS) K2, turn.
Row 3 P3, turn.
Row 4 K3, turn.
Row 5 P4, turn.
Row 6 K4, turn.
Row 7 P5, turn.
Row 8 K5, turn.
Row 9 P6, turn.
Row 10 K6, turn.
Row 11 P7, turn.
Row 12 K7, turn.
Row 13 P8, turn.
Row 14 K8, turn.
Row 15 P9, turn.
Row 16 K9, turn.
Row 17 P10, do *not* turn.
Rep from * for two more triangles—3 Base Triangles made.
Turn.

RH CORNER TRIANGLE
Row 1 (RS) K2, turn.
Row 2 (WS) P2, turn.
Row 3 Inc in first st by knitting into front and back of st, ssk, turn.
Row 4 P3, turn.
Row 5 Inc in first st, k1, ssk, turn.
Row 6 P4, turn.
Row 7 Inc in first st, k2, ssk, turn.
Row 8 P5, turn.
Row 9 Inc in first st, k3, ssk, turn.
Row 10 P6, turn.
Row 11 Inc in first st, k4, ssk, turn.
Row 12 P7, turn.
Row 13 Inc in first st, k5, ssk, turn.
Row 14 P8, turn.
Row 15 Inc in first st, k6, ssk, turn.
Row 16 P9, turn.
Row 17 Inc in first st, k7, ssk, do *not* turn.
The RH Corner Triangle is complete. Leave 10 sts on RH needle.

RS RECTANGLES
*Pick-up row (RS) Pick up and k 10 sts evenly along edge of next triangle/rectangle, turn.
Row 1 (WS) P10, turn.
Row 2 K9, ssk, turn.
Row 3 P10, turn.
*Row 4 K5, yo, ssk, k2, ssk (with last st of rectangle and first st of next triangle/rectangle), turn.
Row 5 P10, turn.
Row 6 K3, k2tog, yo, k1, yo, ssk, k1, ssk, turn.
Row 7 P10, turn.
Row 8 K5, yo, ssk, k2, ssk, turn.
Row 9 P10, turn.
Row 10 K9, ssk, turn.
Row 11 P10, turn.*
Rep between *'s once more.
Row 20 K9, ssk, do *not* turn.
Rep from * across row—2 RS Rectangles made.

LH CORNER TRIANGLE
Pick-up row (RS) Pick up and k 10 sts along edge of last triangle/rectangle, turn.
Row 1 P2tog, p8, turn.
Row 2 K9, turn.
Row 3 P2tog, p7, turn.
Row 4 K8, turn.
Row 5 P2tog, p6, turn.
Row 6 K7, turn.
Row 7 P2tog, p5, turn.
Row 8 K6, turn.
Row 9 P2tog, p4, turn.
Row 10 K5, turn.
Row 11 P2tog, p3, turn.
Row 12 K4, turn.
Row 13 P2tog, p2, turn.
Row 14 K3, turn.
Row 15 P2tog, p1, turn.
Row 16 K2, turn.
Row 17 P2tog, do *not* turn—1 st remains on RH needle.

entre nous
Wristers make great quick gifts and are an easy way to try many of the different stitch patterns in this book. See pages 16 to 73 for dozens of suitable patterns.

WS RECTANGLES
Pick-up row (WS) Pick up and p 9 sts evenly along edge of triangle just worked—10 sts. Turn.
Row 1 (RS) K10, turn.
Row 2 P9, p2tog (with last st of rectangle and first st of next triangle/rectangle), turn.
***Row 3** K4, yo, ssk, k4, turn.
Row 4 P9, p2tog, turn.

Row 5 K2, k2tog, yo, k1, yo, ssk, k3, turn.
Row 6 P9, p2tog, turn.
Row 7 K4, yo, ssk, k4, turn.
Row 8 P9, p2tog, turn.
Row 9 K10, turn.
Row 10 P9, p2tog, turn.*
Rep between *'s once.
Row 19 K10, turn.
Row 20 P9, p2tog, do *not* turn.
Next row (WS) Pick up and p 10 sts evenly along edge of next RS Rectangle.
Rep from row 1 across row—3 WS Rectangles made. Turn.

**Work 1 RH Corner Triangle.
Work 1 row of RS Rectangles. Do *not* turn.
Work 1 LH Corner Triangle.
Work 1 row of WS Rectangles.
Rep from ** until 3 rows of RS Rectangles have been worked, ending with a LH Corner Triangle completed—1 st remains on the needle. Do *not* turn.

END TRIANGLES
***Pick-up row (WS)** Pick up and p 9 sts evenly along edge of triangle just worked—10 sts on RH needle. Turn.
Row 1 (RS) K10, turn.
Row 2 P2tog, p7, p2tog, turn.

Row 3 K9, turn.
Row 4 P2tog, p6, p2tog, turn.
Row 5 K8, turn.
Row 6 P2tog, p5, p2tog, turn.
Row 7 K7, turn.
Row 8 P2tog, p4, p2tog, turn.
Row 9 K6, turn.
Row 10 P2tog, p3, p2tog, turn.
Row 11 K5, turn.
Row 12 P2tog, p2, p2tog, turn.
Row 13 K4, turn.
Row 14 P2tog, p1, p2tog, turn.
Row 15 K3, turn.
Row 16 P2tog, p2tog, turn.
Row 17 K2, turn.
Row 18 P2tog, p2tog, pass first st over 2nd st—1 st remains on RH needle.
Rep from * across row, picking up sts along edge of rectangle instead of triangle. Fasten off.

FINISHING
Block pieces to measurements.
NOTE Cast-on edge forms the hand opening. Fold piece in half widthwise and sew side seam, beginning at End Triangles, for approx 5"/12.5cm. Skip approx 1½"/4cm for thumb opening and sew rem 2"/5cm. ❖

EXPERIENCED

fruit and veggie caps

Three servings of fruits and vegetables will keep your child's head warm and cozy. Change the colors to create his or her garden favorite.

Pumpkin Hat

SIZE
Sized for Child's size 6 months.

FINISHED MEASUREMENTS
Circumference 16"/40.5cm
Height 6½"/16.5cm

MATERIALS
- 1 1¾oz/50g ball (approx 137yd/125m) of Filatura Di Crosa/Tahki•Stacy Charles, Inc. *Zara* (wool) each in #1503 green (A) and #1762 orange (C) ⬛3⬛

- 1 1¾oz/50g ball (approx 137yd/125m) of Filatura Di Crosa/Tahki•Stacy Charles, Inc. *Zara Chiné* (wool) in #805 dark orange (B) ⬛3⬛

- One each sizes 5 and 6 (3.75 and 4mm) circular needle, each 16"/40cm long OR SIZE TO OBTAIN GAUGE

- Stitch marker

GAUGE
18 sts and 28 rows = 4"/10cm over St st using smaller needle.
TAKE TIME TO CHECK GAUGE.

HAT
With larger needle and A, cast on 64 sts. Join, being careful not to twist sts on needles. Place marker for beg of rnd and slip marker every rnd. Knit 8 rnds. Change to smaller needle.

BASE TRIANGLES
*Row 1 (RS) K1, turn.
Row 2 (WS) P1, turn.
Row 3 K2, turn.
Row 4 P2, turn.
Cont in this way working 1 more st every RS row until RS row "k8" has been worked, do *not* turn. Rep from * 7 times more—8 Base Triangles made.
Cut A. Join B. Turn work to WS.

WS RECTANGLES
**With WS facing and RH needle, pick up and p 8 sts down left edge of first Base Triangle. Turn.
Next row (RS) K8, turn.
*Next row (WS) P7, p2tog (the last st of rectangle and first st of Base Triangle), turn.
Next row (RS) K8, turn.
Rep from * until all sts from Base

Triangle are worked, end with last WS row as foll: P7, p2tog (8 sts B on RH needle). Do *not* turn.** Rep from ** to ** for 7 more WS Rectangles—8 rectangles made. Cut B. Join C. Turn work to RS.

RS RECTANGLES
***With RS facing, RH needle and C, pick up and k 8 sts down left side of first WS Rectangle. Turn.
*Next row (WS) P8, turn.
Next row (RS) K7, ssk (first st from RS of Rectangle and first st from WS Rectangle), turn.* Rep from * to * until all sts from WS Rectangle are worked.
End last RS row with K7, ssk,

Pumpkin Hat

do *not* turn.**
Rep from ** to ** until 8 RS Rectangles have been made. The last RS row is k7, ssk, turn.

WS RECTANGLES
NOTE For dec row, when picking up 1 st less, pick up the last 2 sts near the end of the row to avoid a hole in the work.
First dec row (WS) With B, pick up and p 7 sts along rectangle. Work as for WS Rectangle, working 7 sts in every rectangle.
NOTE There will be 8 sts for previous rectangle, and on last WS row, work p6, sssk—7 sts on RH needle.
Cont until 8 WS Rectangles are worked, each with 7 sts.

2ND DEC ROW—RS RECTANGLES
With C, pick up and k 6 sts. Work 1 round of RS Rectangles (8 in total), each 6 sts.

WS RECTANGLES
With B, work 8 WS Rectangles using 5 sts and working in St st.

Clockwise from top:
Eggplant Hat,
Pumpkin Hat and
Strawberry Hat.

RS RECTANGLES

With B, pick up and k 5 sts and work 8 RS Rectangles as foll:

Next row (RS) Pick up and k 5 sts, turn.

Next row (WS) P5, turn.

Next row K4, ssk, turn.

Next row P4, turn.

Next row K4, ssk, turn.

Next row P4 (leave 1 st unworked), turn.

Next row K3, ssk, turn.

Next row P3, turn.

Next row K2, ssk, turn.

Next row P2, turn.

Next row K1, ssk, turn.

Next row P1, turn.

Next row Ssk, do *not* turn—5 sts on RH needle.

Rep for 7 more RS Rectangles—40 sts on needle.

FINISHING

Next rnd (RS) *Ssk; rep from * around—20 sts.

Next rnd (RS) *Ssk; rep from * around—10 sts.

Next rnd (RS) *Ssk; rep from * around—5 sts. Cut B, join A.

I-CORD

*Next row (RS)** K5, sl sts to beg of needle; rep from * until I-cord measures 1"/2.5cm. Bind off. ❖

Eggplant Hat

SIZE

Sized for Child's size 6 months.

FINISHED MEASUREMENTS

Circumference 16"/40.5cm
Height 6½"/16.5cm

MATERIALS

■ 1 1¾oz/50g skein (approx 136.5yd/125m) each of Filatura Di Crosa/Tahki•Stacy Charles, Inc. *Zara* (wool) in #1503 green (A) and #1706 purple (B) ③

■ 1 .88oz/25g skein (approx 328yd/300m) of Filatura Di Crosa/Tahki•Stacy Charles, Inc., *Superior* (cashmere/silk) in #22 lilac (C), used double-stranded. ②

■ One each sizes 5 and 6 (3.75 and 4mm) circular needles each 16"/40cm long OR SIZE TO OBTAIN GAUGE

■ Stitch marker

GAUGE

18 sts and 28 rows = 4"/10cm over St st using smaller needle and *Zara*.
TAKE TIME TO CHECK GAUGE.

NOTE Use 2 strands of *Superior* (C) throughout.

HAT

With larger needle and A, cast on 64 sts. Join, being careful not to twist sts on needles. Place marker for beg of rnd and slip marker every rnd. Knit 8 rnds. Change to smaller needle. Cut A, join B.

BASE TRIANGLES

*Row 1 (RS)** K1, turn.

Row 2 (WS) P1, turn.

Row 3 K2, turn.

Row 4 P2, turn.

Cont in this way working 1 more st every RS row until the RS row "k8" has been worked, do *not* turn.

Rep from * 7 times more—8 Base Triangles made.

Cut B. Join 2 strands C. Turn work to WS.

WS RECTANGLES

**With WS facing, pick up and p 8 sts down left edge of first Base Triangle. Turn.

Next row (RS) K8, turn.

*Next row (WS)** P7, p2tog (the last st of rectangle and first st of Base Triangle), turn.

Next row (RS) K8, turn. Rep from * until all sts from Base Triangle are worked, end with

last WS row as foll: P7, p2tog (8 sts B on RH needle). Do *not* turn.** Rep from ** to ** for 7 more WS Rectangles for a total of 8 rectangles worked. Cut C. Join B. Turn work to RS.

RS RECTANGLES

***With RS facing and B, with RH needle pick up and k 8 sts down left side of first WS Rectangle. Turn.

*Next row (WS)** P8, turn.

Next row (RS) K7, ssk (first st from RS of rectangle and first st from WS rectangle), turn.* Rep from * to * until all sts from WS Rectangle are worked. End last RS row with K7, ssk, do *not* turn.**

Rep from ** to ** until 8 RS Rectangles have been made. The last RS row is k7, ssk, turn.

NOTE For dec row, when picking up 1 st less, pick up the last 2 sts near the end of the row to avoid a hole in the work.

WS RECTANGLES

DEC ROW (WS) With C, pick up and p 7 sts along rectangle. Work as for WS Rectangle, working 7 sts in every rectangle.

NOTE There will be 8 sts for

previous rectangle. On last WS row, work p6, sssk—7 sts on RH needle.

Cont until 8 WS Rectangles are made, each with 7 sts.

RS RECTANGLES

With B, pick up and k 6 sts. Work 8 RS Rectangles using 6 sts each.

LEAVES

With A, work 8 WS Rectangles using 5 sts, working in St st.

RS RECTANGLES

With A, pick up and k 5 sts and work 8 RS Rectangles as foll:

Next row (RS) Pick up and k 5 sts, turn.

Next row (WS) P5, turn.

Next row K4, ssk, turn.

Next row P4, turn.

Next row K4, ssk, turn.

Next row P4 (leave 1 st unworked), turn.

Next row K3, ssk, turn.

Next row P3, turn.

Next row K2, ssk, turn.

Next row P2, turn.

Next row K1, ssk, turn.

Next row P1, turn.

Next row Ssk, do *not* turn—5 sts on RH needle.

Rep for 7 more Leaves—40 sts on needle.

FINISHING

Next rnd (RS) *Ssk; rep from * around—20 sts.

Next rnd (RS) *Ssk; rep from * around—10 sts.

Next rnd (RS) *Ssk; rep from * around—5 sts.

I-CORD

*Next row (RS) K5, sl sts to beg of needle; rep from * until I-cord measures 1"/2.5cm. Bind off. ❖

Strawberry Hat

SIZE

Sized for a Child's size 6 months.

FINISHED MEASUREMENTS

Circumference 16"/40.5cm
Height 6½"/16.5cm

MATERIALS

■ 1 1¾oz/50g ball (approx 136.5yd/125m) of Filatura Di Crosa/Tahki•Stacy Charles, Inc. *Zara* (wool) each in #1493 dark red (A), #1466 red (B) and #1503 green (C) (3)

■ One each sizes 5 and 6 (3.75 and 4mm) circular needle, each 16"/40cm long OR SIZE TO OBTAIN GAUGE

■ Stitch marker

GAUGES

■ 18 sts and 28 rows = 4"/10cm over St st using larger needle.

■ 20 sts and 48 rows = 4"/10cm over garter st using smaller needle.

TAKE TIME TO CHECK GAUGES.

HAT

With larger needle and A, cast on 64 sts. Join, being careful not to twist sts on needle. Place marker for beg of rnd and slip marker every rnd. K 8 rnds. Change to smaller needle.

BASE TRIANGLES

(worked in knit garter st)

*Row 1 (RS) K1, turn.

Row 2 (WS) K1, turn.

Row 3 K2, turn.

Row 4 K2, turn.

Cont in this way, knitting 1 more st every RS row until the RS row "k8" has been worked, do *not* turn.

Rep from * 7 times more—8 Base Triangles made. Cut A. Join B.

note

To get the textured "berry" look, I used garter stitch for the body and stockinette stitch for the brim and leaves.

Turn work to WS.

WS RECTANGLES

(worked in purl garter st)

**With WS facing, pick up and p 8 sts down left edge of first Base Triangle. Turn.

Next row (RS) P8, turn.

*Next row (WS) P7, p2tog (the last st of rectangle and first st of Base Triangle), turn.

Next row (RS) P8, turn. Rep from * until all sts from Base Triangle are worked, end with last WS row as foll: P7, p2tog (8 sts B on RH needle). Do *not* turn.**

Rep from ** to ** for 7 more WS Rectangles—8 rectangles made. Cut B. Join A. Turn work to RS.

RS RECTANGLES

(worked in knit garter st)

***With RS facing and A, with RH needle pick up and k 8 sts down left side of first WS Rectangle (pick up in the bumps). Turn.

*Next row (WS) K8, turn.

Next row (RS) K7, ssk (first st from RS of rectangle and first st from WS Rectangle), turn.* Rep from * to * until all sts from WS Rectangle are worked. End last RS row with K7, ssk, do *not* turn.***

Rep from *** to *** until 8 RS Rectangles have been made. The

last RS row is k7, ssk, turn.
NOTE For dec row, when picking up 1 st less, pick up last 2 sts near the end of the row to avoid a hole in the work.

WS RECTANGLES

Dec row (WS) With B, pick up and p 7 sts along rectangle. Work as for WS Rectangle, working 7 sts in every rectangle.
NOTE There will be 8 sts for previous rectangle, and on last WS row, work p6, sssk—7 sts on RH needle.
Cont until 8 WS rectangles are worked, each with 7 sts.

RS RECTANGLES

With A, pick up and k 6 sts. Work a round of RS Rectangles (8 in total) each 6 sts.

LEAVES

With C, work 8 WS Rectangles using 5 sts and working in St st.

RS RECTANGLES

With C, pick up and k 5 sts and work 8 RS Rectangles as foll:
Next row (RS) Pick up and k 5 sts, turn.
Next row (WS) P5, turn.
Next row K4, ssk, turn.
Next row P4, turn.
Next row K4, ssk, turn.

Next row P4 (leave 1 st unworked), turn.
Next row K3, ssk, turn.
Next row P3, turn.
Next row K2, ssk, turn.
Next row P2, turn.
Next row K1, ssk, turn.
Next row P1, turn.
Next row Ssk, do *not* turn—5 sts on RH needle.
Rep for 7 more Leaves—40 sts on needle.

FINISHING

Next rnd (RS) *Ssk; rep from * around—20 sts.
Next rnd (RS) *Ssk; rep from * around—10 sts.
Next rnd (RS) *Ssk; rep from * around—5 sts.

I-CORD

*Next row (RS) K5, sl sts to beg of needle; rep from * until I-cord measures 1"/2.5cm. Bind off. ❖

Eggplant Hat

Strawberry Hat

**Work 1 RH Triangle.
Work 24 (26, 27) RS Rectangles.
Work 1 LH Triangle.
Work 25 (27, 28) WS Rectangles.
Rep from ** 3 times more.

END TRIANGLES
Row 1 (RS) K1, turn.
Row 2 (WS) K1, turn.
Rows 3 and 4 K2, turn.
Rows 5 and 6 K3, turn.
Rows 7 and 8 K4, turn.
Rows 9 and 10 K5, turn.
Rows 11 and 12 K6, turn.
Rows 13 and 14 K7, turn.
Rows 15 and 16 K8, turn.
Next row (RS) Bind off 7 sts—1
st remains. Do *not* turn.
*Pick-up row (RS)** Pick up
and k 7 sts evenly along
edge of next rectangle—8 sts
on RH needle.
Row 1 (WS) K8, turn.
Row 2 Ssk, k5, k2tog, turn.
Row 3 K7, turn.
Row 4 Ssk, k4, k2tog, turn.
Row 5 K6, turn.
Row 6 Ssk, k3, k2tog, turn.
Row 7 K5, turn.
Row 8 Ssk, k2, k2tog, turn.
Row 9 K4, turn.
Row 10 Ssk, k1, k2tog, turn.
Row 11 K3, turn.
Row 12 Ssk, k2tog, turn.
Row 13 K2, turn.
Row 14 K1, k2tog, turn.
Row 15 K2, turn.
Row 16 K3tog, do *not* turn—
1 st remains.

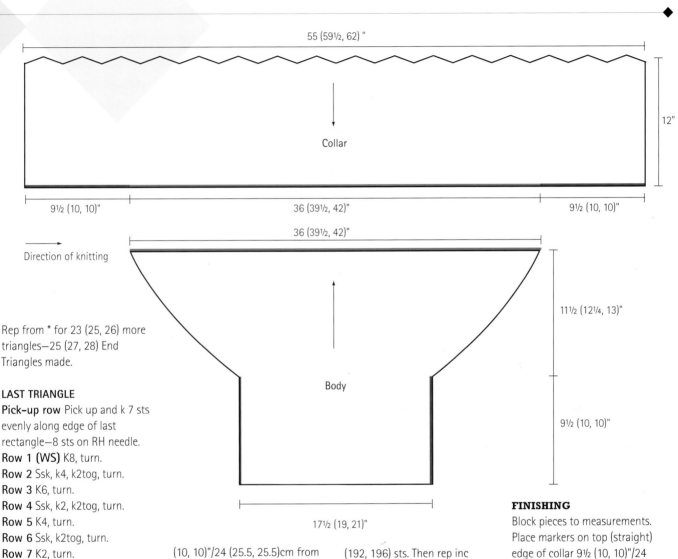

55 (59½, 62) "

Collar

12"

9½ (10, 10)" — **36 (39½, 42)"** — **9½ (10, 10)"**

36 (39½, 42)"

Direction of knitting

Body

11½ (12¼, 13)"

9½ (10, 10)"

17½ (19, 21)"

Rep from * for 23 (25, 26) more triangles—25 (27, 28) End Triangles made.

LAST TRIANGLE
Pick-up row Pick up and k 7 sts evenly along edge of last rectangle—8 sts on RH needle.
Row 1 (WS) K8, turn.
Row 2 Ssk, k4, k2tog, turn.
Row 3 K6, turn.
Row 4 Ssk, k2, k2tog, turn.
Row 5 K4, turn.
Row 6 Ssk, k2tog, turn.
Row 7 K2, turn.
Row 8 K2tog. Fasten off.

BODY
Cast on 92 (100, 110) sts. Work in garter st for 104 (110, 110) rows. Piece measures approx 9½

(10, 10)"/24 (25.5, 25.5)cm from beg. Place markers on both edges of piece.
Inc row (RS) K2, M1, k to last 2 sts, M1, k2—94 (102, 112) sts. Rep inc row every other row 38 (45, 42) times more—170

(192, 196) sts. Then rep inc row every 4th row 10 (8, 12) times—190 (208, 220) sts. Work 11 rows even. Piece measures approx 11½ (12¼, 13)"/29 (31, 33)cm above markers. Bind off loosely.

FINISHING
Block pieces to measurements. Place markers on top (straight) edge of collar 9½ (10, 10)"/24 (25.5, 25.5)cm in from each side edge. Sew upper edge of Body to collar between markers. Fold garment and sew rem edges of top of collar to side edges of Body (see schematic). ❖

INTERMEDIATE

accent on angora shawl

Outlining the entrelac rectangles in fluffy angora yarn adds a subtle contrast to Laura Bryant's luscious wrap.

SIZE
Sized for Small (Large). Shown in size Small.

FINISHED MEASUREMENTS
Approximately 16" x 60 (80)"/40cm x 152.5 (203)cm

MATERIALS
- 6 (8) 2oz/57g balls (each approx 118yd/108m) of Prism Yarns *Symphony* (merino/cashmere/nylon) in copper penny (A) 🔳
- 2 (3) 1oz/28g balls (each approx 90yd/82m) of Prism Yarns *Angora* (angora) in highlands (B) 🔳
- One pair size 8 (5mm) needles OR SIZE TO OBTAIN GAUGE
- Size G/6 (4mm) crochet hook

GAUGE
18 sts and 26 rows = 4"/10cm over St st using size 8 (5mm) needles.
TAKE TIME TO CHECK GAUGE.

SHAWL
BASE RECTANGLES
*With B, cast on 12 sts.
Row 1 (RS) K12, turn.
Row 2 (WS) K12, turn.
Join A and work as foll, carrying B along side of rectangle:
Rows 3–22 K12, turn. Cut A after last row.
Rows 23 and 24 With B, k12, turn.
Rep from * for 3 more rectangles—4 Rectangles made. Do *not* cut A on last rectangle.

RH CORNER TRIANGLE
Row 1 (RS) With A, k2, turn.
Row 2 P2, turn.
Row 3 Inc in first st by knitting into front and back of st, ssk (with last st of triangle and first st of next rectangle), turn.
Row 4 P3, turn.
Row 5 Inc in first st, k1, ssk, turn.
Row 6 P4, turn.
Row 7 Inc in first st, k2, ssk, turn.
Row 8 P5, turn.
Row 9 Inc in first st, k3, ssk, turn.

Row 10 P6, turn.
Row 11 Inc in first st, k4, ssk, turn.
Row 12 P7, turn.
Row 13 Inc in first st, k5, ssk, turn.
Row 14 P8, turn.
Row 15 Inc in first st, k6, ssk, turn.
Row 16 P9, turn.
Row 17 Inc in first st, k7, ssk, turn.
Row 18 P10, turn. Change to B (do not break A).
Row 19 Inc in first st, k8, ssk, turn.
Row 20 P11, turn.
Row 21 Inc in first st, k9 (carrying A along back of work), ssk, do *not* turn.

RS RECTANGLES
*Pick-up row (RS) With B, pick up and k 12 sts evenly along edge of next rectangle, turn.
Row 1 P12, turn. Change to A.
Row 2 K11, ssk (with last st of rectangle and first st of next rectangle), turn.
Row 3 P12, turn.
Rows 4–21 Rep rows 2 and 3 nine times. Change to B (do *not* cut A).

notes

1 Each rectangle begins and ends with B; centers are worked with A.
2 When working the A sections, carry B along side edge until needed again as foll: At beg of RS rows, lay B strand over A strand.
3 On St st rectangles, sometimes A will need to be carried loosely along WS of work on a B row, so it will be in position for next square. Don't carry A on garter rectangles or it will show on RS of work; instead, break yarn and rejoin for each rectangle.
4 Use cable cast-on throughout.

Row 22 K11, ssk, turn.
Row 23 P12, turn.
Row 24 K11 (carrying A along back of work), ssk, do *not* turn. Rep from * for 2 more rectangles—3 RS Rectangles made.

LH CORNER TRIANGLE

Pick-up row (RS) With B, pick up and k 12 sts along edge of last rectangle, turn.
Row 1 P2tog, p10, turn. Change to A.
Row 2 K11, turn.
Row 3 P2tog, p9, turn.
Row 4 K10, turn.
Row 5 P2tog, p8, turn.
Row 6 K9, turn.
Row 7 P2tog, p7, turn.
Row 8 K8, turn.
Row 9 P2tog, p6, turn.
Row 10 K7, turn.
Row 11 P2tog, p5, turn.
Row 12 K6, turn.
Row 13 P2tog, p4, turn.
Row 14 K5, turn.
Row 15 P2tog, p3, turn.
Row 16 K4, turn.
Row 17 P2tog, p2, turn.
Row 18 K3, turn.
Row 19 P2tog, p1, turn.
Row 20 K2, turn.
Row 21 P2tog, do *not* turn—1 st remains.

WS RECTANGLES

Pick-up row (WS) With B, pick up and p 11 sts evenly along edge of triangle just worked—12 sts on RH needle, turn.
***Row 1** K12, turn.
Row 2 P11 (carrying A along front of work), p2tog (with last st of rectangle and first st of next triangle/rectangle), turn. Change to A.
Row 3 K12, turn.
Row 4 P11, p2tog, turn.
Rows 5–22 Rep rows 3 and 4 nine times. Change to B (do *not* cut A).
Row 23 K12, turn.
Row 24 P11, p2tog, do *not* turn.
Next row (WS) Pick up and p 12 sts evenly along edge of next RS Rectangle.
Rep from * for 3 more rectangles (omitting last pick-up row after last rectangle)—4 WS Rectangles made. Turn.

**Work 1 RH Triangle.
Work 3 RS Rectangles.
Work 1 LH Triangle.
Work 4 WS Rectangles.
Rep from ** 10 (14) times more.

Work 1 RH Triangle. Work 3 RS Rectangles. Work 1 LH Triangle. Cut A.

END RECTANGLES

***Pick-up row (WS)** With B, pick up and p 11 sts evenly along edge of triangle/rectangle just worked—12 sts on RH needle, turn.
Row 1 K12, turn.
Row 2 K11, k2tog, turn. Join A and work as foll:
Row 3 K12, turn.
Row 4 K11, k2tog, turn.
Rows 5–22 Rep rows 3 and 4 nine times. Change to B (cut A).
Row 23 K12, turn.
Next row (WS) Bind off sts knitwise, working k2tog before binding off last st, do *not* turn. Rep from * for 3 more rectangles—4 End Rectangles made. Fasten off.

FINISHING

With RS facing, crochet hook and B, work 1 row reverse single crochet along upper and lower (sawtooth) edges. ❖

entre nous

The technique used here to outline the entrelac rectangles in a different yarn could easily be used for other projects. Try smaller rectangles for a different look.

To achieve the sawtooth edge, the Base Triangles were substituted with Base Rectangles.

Figuring Out Gauge

Measuring gauge in entrelac is not quite the same as measuring gauge in traditional flat knitting because entrelac is worked on the diagonal. As with any knitting project, you must get your gauge before beginning to knit. Here's how.

First knit a flat swatch using the stitch pattern and yarn for your project. Once you get a gauge you are happy with, use the same size needle and yarn and work an entrelac swatch in the same pattern with at least two Base Triangles and two Rectangles (the swatches shown here have three Base Triangles). Measure the entire width and length of the swatch and divide that number by the number of triangles (for the stitches) and the number of rectangles (for the rows). For example, one of our swatches measures 6" and three triangles wide by 4" and two rectangles high—that is one triangle measures 2" wide and one rectangle measures 2" high. Therefore if you want to make a scarf that is 8" wide by 40" long, you need four triangles (8 divided by 2) and twenty rectangles (40 divided by 2).

For an item that must be a specific size, the directions often include two gauges, one in the stitch pattern used (for example, seed) and the other giving the measurements of two or three triangles and a row of rectangles. ❖

Here the yarn and needle size are the same for each swatch, but casting on a different number of stitches for each Base Triangle (e.g., 4, 6, 8 or 10 stitches) changes the size of the swatches.

In the swatches above, the same number of stitches were cast on for each, but different yarns and needle sizes were used, resulting in different-size swatches.

Abbreviations & More

Abbreviations

approx	approximately	rem	remain(s)(ing)
beg	begin(ning)	rep	repeat
CC	contrasting color	RH	right-hand
ch	chain	RS	right side(s)
cm	centimeter(s)	rnd(s)	round(s)
cn	cable needle	SKP	slip 1, knit 1, pass slip stitch over—one stitch has been decreased
cont	continu(e)(ing)		
dec	decreas(e)(ing)		
dpn(s)	double-pointed needle(s)	SK2P	slip 1, knit 2 together, pass slip stitch over the knit 2 together—two stitches have been decreased
foll	follow(s)(ing)		
g	gram(s)		
inc	increas(e)(ing)		
k	knit		
k1fb	knit into the front and back of a stitch—one stitch has been increased	S2KP	slip 2 stitches together, knit 1, pass 2 slip stitches over knit 1
		sc	single crochet
k2tog	knit 2 stitches together—one stitch has been decreased	sl	slip
		sl st	slip stitch
		spp	slip, purl, pass sl st over
LH	left-hand	ssk (ssp)	slip, slip, knit (purl)
lp(s)	loop(s)	sssk	slip, slip, slip, knit
m	meter(s)	st(s)	stitch(es)
mm	millimeter(s)	St st	stockinette stitch
MC	main color	tbl	through back loop(s)
M1	make one stitch	tog	together
oz	ounce(s)	WS	wrong side(s)
p	purl	wyib	with yarn in back
p1fb	purl into front and back of a stitch—one stitch has been increased	wyif	with yarn in front
		yd	yard(s)
		yo	yarn over needle
pat(s)	pattern(s)	*	repeat directions following * as many times as indicated
pm	place marker		
psso	pass slip stitch(es) over		
p2tog	purl two stitches together—one stitch has been decreased	[ ]	repeat directions inside brackets as many times as indicated

Standard Yarn Weight System

Categories of yarn, gauge ranges, and recommended needle and hook sizes

Yarn Weight Symbol & Category Names	0 Lace	1 Super Fine	2 Fine	3 Light	4 Medium	5 Bulky	6 Super Bulky
Type of Yarns in Category	Fingering 10 count crochet thread	Sock, Fingering, Baby	Sport, Baby	DK, Light Worsted	Worsted, Afghan, Aran	Chunky, Craft, Rug	Bulky, Roving
Knit Gauge Range* in Stockinette Stitch to 4 inches	33–40** sts	27–32 sts	23–26 sts	21–24 sts	16–20 sts	12–15 sts	6–11 sts
Recommended Needle in Metric Size Range	1.5–2.25 mm	2.25–3.25 mm	3.25–3.75 mm	3.75–4.5 mm	4.5–5.5 mm	5.5–8 mm	8 mm and larger
Recommended Needle U.S. Size Range	000 to 1	1 to 3	3 to 5	5 to 7	7 to 9	9 to 11	11 and larger
Crochet Gauge* Ranges in Single Crochet to 4 inch	32–42 double crochets**	21–32 sts	16–20 sts	12–17 sts	11–14 sts	8–11 sts	5–9 sts
Recommended Hook in Metric Size Range	Steel*** 1.6–1.4mm Regular hook 2.25 mm	2.25–3.5 mm	3.5–4.5 mm	4.5–5.5 mm	5.5–6.5 mm	6.5–9 mm	9 mm and larger
Recommended Hook U.S. Size Range	Steel*** 6, 7, 8 Regular hook B–1	B–1 to E–4	E–4 to 7	7 to I–9	I–9 to K–10½	K–10½ to M–13	M–13 and larger

* GUIDELINES ONLY: The above reflect the most commonly used gauges and needle or hook sizes for specific yarn categories.

** Lace weight yarns are usually knitted or crocheted on larger needles and hooks to create lacy, openwork patterns. Accordingly, a gauge range is difficult to determine. Always follow the gauge stated in your pattern.

*** Steel crochet hooks are sized differently from regular hooks--the higher the number, the smaller the hook, which is the reverse of regular hook sizing.

This Standards & Guidelines booklet and downloadable symbol artwork are available at: **YarnStandards.com**

Skill Levels

BEGINNER
For knitters who have some knitting experience but are trying entrelac for the first time.

EASY
For knitters who have mastered the basic entrelac technique and are ready to move on to patterns with more involved stitches.

INTERMEDIATE
For knitters with experience working intricate stitches and some shaping and finishing.

EXPERIENCED
For knitters able to work patterns with complicated shaping and finishing.

resources

ARTYARNS
39 Westmoreland Avenue
White Plains, NY 10606
www.artyarns.com

CASCADE YARNS
1224 Andover Park East
Tukwila, WA 98188
www.cascadeyarns.com

CLASSIC ELITE YARNS
122 Western Avenue
Lowell, MA 01851
www.classiceliteyarns.com

DMC
10 Basin Drive, Suite 130
Kearny, NJ 07032
www.dmc-usa.com

FIESTA YARNS
5401 San Diego Ave. NE
Albuquerque, NM 87113
www.fiestayarns.com

FILATURA DI CROSA
Dist. by Tahki•Stacy Charles, Inc.

KNITTING FEVER INC. (KFI)
P.O. Box 336
315 Bayview Avenue
Amityville, NY 11701
www.knittingfever.com

KOIGU WOOL DESIGNS
P.O. Box 158
Chatsworth, ON N0H 1G0
Canada
www.koigu.com

LOUET NORTH AMERICA
808 Commerce Park Drive
Ogdensburg, NY 13669
www.louet.com

MOKUBA
55 West 39th Street
New York, NY 10018
www.mokubany.com

NASHUA HANDKNITS
Dist. by Westminster Fibers, Inc.
www.nashuaknits.com

NORO
Dist. by Knitting Fever Inc.

PRISM
www.prismyarn.com

ROWAN
Dist. by Westminster Fibers, Inc.
www.knitrowan.com

SKACEL COLLECTION
P.O. Box 88110
Seattle, WA 98138
www.skacelknitting.com

TAHKI•STACY CHARLES, INC.
70-30 80th Street, Building 36
Ridgewood, NY 11385
www.tahkistacycharles.com

TAHKI YARNS
Dist. by Tahki•Stacy Charles, Inc.

WESTMINSTER FIBERS, INC.
165 Ledge Street
Nashua, NH 03060
www.nashuaknits.com

**YARNS USED IN SWATCH
GLOSSARY** (pp. 16–73)

Cashsoft DK from Rowan Yarns:
pp. 19–34, 36 (top), 40–49

Superior from Filatura Di
Crosa/Tahki•Stacy Charles, Inc.:
pp. 36 (bottom), 37–39, 64

Lana from Tahki Yarns/Tahki•Stacy
Charles, Inc.: pp. 35, 57, 61

Zara from Filatura Di
Crosa/Tahki•Stacy Charles, Inc.:
pp. 50–52, 56, 60, 70

Cascade 220 from Cascade Yarns:
pp. 53–55, 58–59

Montera from Classic Elite Yarns:
pp. 62, 65, 66 (top right),
67 (top left), 72 (top)

Donegal Tweed from Tahki Yarns/
Tahki•Stacy Charles, Inc.: p. 63

Ritratto from S. Charles/
Tahki•Stacy Charles, Inc.: pp. 64, 67
(top right)

Sahara from S. Charles/Tahki•Stacy
Charles, Inc.: pp. 66 (top left),
72 (bottom)

African Bead Ball from Be Sweet:
pp. 66 (top right), 67 (top left)

Rock Star Rattan from Tilli Tomas:
p. 66 (bottom)

Tempo from Filatura Di Crosa/
Tahki•Stacy Charles, Inc.:
p. 67 (bottom)

Painter's Palette Premium Merino
from Koigu Wool Designs: p. 68

Nepal Print by Tahki Yarns/Tahki•
Stacy Charles, Inc.: p. 69 (top left)

Iro from Noro Yarns: p. 69 (right)

Rain from Tahki Yarns/Tahki•Stacy
Charles, Inc.: pp. 71, 73

index

entre nous

■ The piece on the cover is knit in *Magnolia* by Classic Elite Yarns. The needles were provided by Signature Needle Arts.

■ The needles shown on pages 4–15 are from ChiaoGoo.

acknowledgments

This book would not have been possible without the support of so many wonderful people around me. I would like to thank Trisha Malcolm for encouraging my creativity, and Art Joinnides for his never-failing belief in me.

My deepest appreciation is to Carla Scott, whose amazing technical expertise, excellent humor and devoted friendship mean so much to me.

I am indebted to my fellow staff at *Vogue Knitting* and Sixth&Spring Books—in particular Michelle Bredeson, Diane Lamphron, Wendy Williams, Renee Lorion, Joe Vior and Sarah Leibowitz—an immensely talented and hard-working group of people.

Special thanks to Joni Coniglio, Harriet Elliott, Pam Grushkin, and Myra Savage, and to the many yarn companies for their contributions. I am grateful to the designers whose work is included: Laura Bryant, Brian Kohler, Svetlana Kudrevich, Kathy Merrick, Kay Neiderlitz, Theresa Schabes, Lori Steinberg and the late Barbara Venishnick. Thanks to all our talented photographers and to those who made the production of this book happen.

The support and patience of my family kept me knitting sanely for months on end. Thanks to my husband, Russell, and my daughters, Shona and Annabelle.

sixth&spring books

Executive Editor
Carla Scott

Managing Editor
Wendy Williams

Senior Editor
Michelle Bredeson

Art Director
Diane Lamphron

Page Layout
Janeen Bellafiore

Instructions Editor
Joni Coniglio

Instructions Proofreader
Salli Sternberg

Yarn Editor
Renee Lorion

Copy Editor
Kristina Sigler

Technical Illustrations
Uli Monch

Model Photography
Rose Callahan

Still Life Photography
Marcus Tullis
Jack Deutsch Studio

Stylist
Sarah Liebowitz

Hair and Makeup
Joe J. Simon for Giorgio Armani
Beauty/ArtistsByTimothy
Priano.com

Vice President, Publisher
Trisha Malcolm

Creative Director
Joe Vior

Production Manager
David Joinnides

President
Art Joinnides